YOU'LL RUIN YOUR DINNER
SWEET MEMORIES FROM IRISH CHILDHOOD

YOU'LL RUIN YOUR DINNER

SWEET MEMORIES
FROM IRISH CHILDHOOD

DAMIAN CORLESS

HACHETTE
BOOKS
IRELAND

First published in 2011 by Hachette Books Ireland
First published in paperback in 2012 by Hachette Books Ireland

Copyright © 2011 Damian Corless

1

The right of Damian Corless to be identified as the Author of the Work
has been asserted by him in accordance with the Copyright, Designs and
Patents Act 1988.

A CIP catalogue record for this title is available from the British Library.

ISBN 978 1 444 72603 9

Typeset in Baskerville and Shadowed Serif by Bookends.
Cover and interior design by AmpVisual.com

Printed and bound in Great Britain by Clays Ltd, St Ives plc.

Hachette Books Ireland policy is to use papers that are natural,
renewable and recyclable products and made from wood grown in
sustainable forests. The logging and manufacturing processes are
expected to conform to the environmental regulations of the country of
origin.

Hachette Books Ireland
8 Castlecourt Centre
Castleknock
Dublin 15, Ireland

A division of Hachette UK Ltd
338 Euston Road
London NW1 3BH
www.hachette.ie

For dedicated sweet fans
Max 'Big Truck' Corless (age 2) and Caitlin Norp (age 1)

Acknowledgements

Thanks to Ciara Considine, Faith O'Grady, Breda Purdue, Joanna Smyth, Nicola Eagles, Linda Spencer, Deirdre Harte and others too numerous to mention.

The author and publishers would like to thank Cadbury's, HB, Lemon's, Mars Ireland, Davison & Associates, Irish Picture Library/Fr FM Browne SJ Collection, the National Library of Ireland and Getty Images for kind permission to reproduce images.

The publishers have endeavoured to contact all copyright holders of illustrative material featured within the book and encourage copyright holders of any material not credited to make contact on info@hachette.ie.

CONTENTS

INTRODUCTION

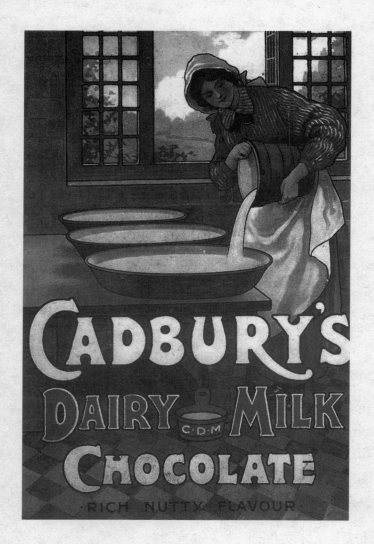

The Irish are the biggest chocolate eaters in the world, chomping through some eleven kilograms per person each year. We're also high-fliers in the planet's premier league for confectionery in general.

I'm no exception. At least, I wasn't. In the Corless household of my childhood, the finger-wagging phrase 'you'll ruin your dinner' featured in the top five most frequently uttered phrases just behind 'brush your teeth', 'say your prayers', 'do your homework' and 'stop doing that'.

My dad, Martin, was a telephone engineer. Every time he returned home from a work outing to Cork, he'd have a round wooden box of Hadji Bey's highly exotic Turkish Delight with big chunks of sugar dusted jelly which were a highlight of my childhood.

The lowlight of my childhood was going to school, and I put up heroic resistance. The local national school was a prefabricated Stalag that squatted at the foot of a hill. At the top of the hill, at the halfway point between our house and the school, was a poky dim and dingy sweetshop called The Little Owl. For me, The Little Owl would come to represent the point of no return between happiness and misery.

When I was four-and-a-half my mother strapped my schoolbag to my back, took a firm grip of my little hand and dragged me on the short walk (which for me was a trail of tears) to attend my first day at school. As we neared The Little Owl, I decided it was now or never – I broke her grip and ran like the wind to find a hiding place in our front garden.

Indulgent and loving, she relented, and I'd won a reprieve.

A year later, as that dreaded date in September approached again, I came up with a cunning plan – I'd do exactly the same again.

And I did.

And it worked!

And that's how I lived out every young child's dream and avoided going to school until I was getting on for the advanced age of seven. After that, The Little Owl became a regular stopover on my walk home from school, where a few of us would pool our pennies to buy a quarter-pound of bull's eyes weighed out into a paper bag or greaseproof cone.

Other treasured memories include savouring Sherbet Fountains on a trip up the road from my home in Dublin to Drogheda where we were mesmerised, and a little repulsed, by the sight of the mummified head of the Catholic martyr Oliver Plunkett. I vividly remember the fizz of the sherbet and the plastic doll bought by my mother, Kay, for my sister, Mary. Stamped on it were the words 'Made in China'. Mary went into school the next day and told her friends, with impeccable logic, that the Corless family had spent the previous Sunday afternoon visiting China.

The memories don't stop there. Back from a brief trip to the west of Ireland, my parents gushed about how they'd met the burly American actor and singer Burl Ives

in a pub. In our household, this was bigger than meeting The Beatles. A vinyl album of Ives' children's songs was a mainstay of the record deck, and my favourite, along with 'There Was An Old Woman Who Swallowed A Fly', was 'Big Rock Candy Mountain'.

'Big Rock Candy Mountain' was about an American drifter's notion of paradise. The original version referred to cigarette trees, lakes of whiskey and other grown-up things, but Ive's version concentrated on the lemonade springs and the soda fountains, which was good enough for us.

We were prepared to blur the line between real sweets and the ones you could make up with a little imagination and empty pockets. Perhaps the worst idea we had involved mixing some Mi-Wadi orange concentrate and Andrews Liver Salts to make a concoction that was our own version of the Fanta fizzy drink.

Predictably, it lacked the finesse of the factory-made pop, but there were worse episodes.

On a holiday visit to Bunratty Castle, the family had a bite of lunch in the teashop. There were mini-pats of butter on the table, and I cruelly informed my younger sister, Mary, that these were caramel sweets. She popped one in her mouth, chewed, and went into convulsions of nausea.

As she recently reminded me, 'After that, I had a fear of butter. I ate dry bread for years.'

Karma meted out my comeuppance a couple of years later on a school trip to Belgium. I still get a toxic taste in my mouth when I relive how I greedily gulped down a lump of something I assumed to be a caramel sweet dusted with icing sugar. It was Brie cheese, which was quite a shock to a palate brought up on Calvita cheese.

I'll spare you further detail, but my taste buds were traumatised for life.

છ છ છ છ

There are historical and geographical reasons why the Irish are such big sweet eaters. For centuries, neighbouring Britain was the hub of the world's sugar trade, and Ireland got the spin-off of cheap and plentiful sweetmeats.

As a nation, our real love affair with chocolate and sweets began around the start of the twentieth century, when large numbers of people began moving from the countryside to the towns and cities. The link between the two is no coincidence. The diet of the urban worker and the urban household often lacked the nutrition of their rural counterparts and sweets and chocolates filled that gap. From the 1930s, chocolate and ice cream were marketed for their nutritional food value. As late as the cusp of the 1960s, Cadbury's ran an ad campaign featuring a pooped nurse, urging wilting workers to

'Bridge That Gap' with a bar of Dairy Milk. The promise was that one bar of Dairy Milk was 'worth one glass of milk and two poached eggs in food value'.

Several generations on, we no longer need sweets and chocolates to boost meagre diets, but, by now, the sweet tooth has become embedded in our DNA.

As we shall see, Irish confectionery also has a DNA that's unique to this island. To our east, the signature chocolate of continental Europe is super-smooth and not too sweet. To the west, American chocolate is more chalky and gritty and also less sweet. The British like their chocolate creamier and sweeter, but Irish chocolate is the richest and creamiest in the world. The same can be said of Irish ice cream. In addition, there were a wide variety of uniquely Irish boiled sweets as recently as the

SWEET MEMORIES
EDDIE KAVANAGH, KAVANAGH'S SWEETSHOP,
AUNGIER STREET, DUBLIN

When I was a kid in the 1970s, after Easter my father would break up any unsold Easter eggs and sell them loose as broken chocolate. For kids, it was a very popular source of cheap chocolate which was sold by the quarter pound. My father also had loads of broken Kit-Kat which was sold in the same way. The likes of Cadbury's and Rowntree's had loads of seconds which came off the production line in odd shapes and sizes. Today, they destroy them, but back then they had all these small outlets that would sell them broken. If a factory guy dropped a box of Peggy's legs, the sticks would tend to crack and break, so you got them that way too.

1970s, when the twenty-six counties ceased to be an independent republic of sweet-making.

The early decades of the twentieth century were a Golden Age for the Irish sweetshop, when most towns would have at least one store dedicated to the sale of confectionery, and Dublin's Grafton Street was a wide-eyed children's wonderland of bewitching window displays. Roald Dahl, author of *Charlie and the Chocolate Factory*, captured that sense of wonder when he wrote of his own childhood: 'The sweetshop in Llandaff in the year 1923 was the very centre of our lives. To us, it was what a bar is to a drunk, or a church is to a bishop. Without it there would have been little to live for.'

I was drawn to write this book by two questions.

How and why did the traditional Irish sweetshop disappear, and how and why has it now made a remarkable reappearance in the past few years? (Strictly speaking, that may count as four questions.)

The Clery's department store on O'Connell Street, which sits opposite the old Confectioners' Hall established in 1842, has recently opened an old-style window display of loose sweets.

But Clery's is following a trend, not setting one.

Retro sweetshops are opening for business up and down the country, where shopkeepers lovingly weigh out loose bull's eyes, clove drops and other lines which were on the endangered list not so long ago.

The retro sweet boom is happening far beyond these shores, thanks largely to the rapid growth of online sweetshops, but that's something for others to write about.

This is a uniquely Irish story.

CHAPTER ONE

1900–1930
WINDOWS OF WONDER

The Easter Egg Rising

Dublin, April 1916. As the Easter Rising raged in the capital, and a small band of rebels took up arms for Irish freedom, a considerably greater number of citizens had their sights set on a less ambitious, more short-term type of liberation.

They were Dublin's willing rabble of looters.

Along the swanky shopping mile from Parnell Square on the north of the Liffey to St Stephen's Green on the southside, the crowds seized upon the uprising as a licence to pillage.

The author James Stephens was an eye-witness. He wrote that after the first twenty-four hours of revolt, which had ignited on Easter Monday, the capital's shop fronts were in smithereens. He testified: 'The shops attacked were mainly haberdashers, shoe shops and sweetshops. Very many sweetshops were raided, and until the end of the Rising, sweetshops were the favourite mark of the looters.'

Stephens' claim that sweetshops were the chief target of looters is borne out by newspaper reports, which note that chocolates, toffees and boxes of biscuits topped the lists of items stolen, with toys, fruit, hats and tobacco amongst the other popular takeaways.

One of the reasons sweetshops headed the list is because quality sweets in 1916, or 1926 or 1936 for that matter, were far more glamorous and expensive than they are today.

Another reason was that they were simply there, flaunting themselves in eye-watering displays, just begging to be smash'n'grabbed.

Dublin's city centre was a place where sapping hunger and grinding poverty sat cheek-by-jowl with conspicuous wealth. The main streets were dotted with beguiling sweetshops, each with elaborate window displays showcasing the latest chocolates, toffees, sugared fruits and other mouth-watering lines from Britain and the continent. With advertising in its infancy, these dazzling window displays were an entertainment in themselves, lighting up the drab streets, and there were regular competitions to name the best in the capital and in the other main cities.

Big department stores would usually have a window given over to an elaborate display, and vied for the coveted best-in-show awards. Like the theatre or the concert hall, these shows had their reviewers. One wrote approvingly of the display mounted by Switzer's of Grafton Street: 'It is a well-thought-out window, artistic in its simplicity.'

So when the looters went on the rampage, it was no surprise the glittering sweetshops were first for the ransacking.

Stephens wrote: 'Possibly most of the looters are children who are having the sole gorge of their lives. They have tasted sweet stuffs they had never toothed before, and will never taste again in this life, and, until they die, the insurrection of 1916 will have a sweet savour for them.'

The looters, adult and children, whisked away

whatever Easter eggs had been left unsold on Easter Monday. Most would never have laid hands on a chocolate egg before – for all but the most privileged Irish children, an Easter egg would have been a painted hen or duck egg.

Chocolate Easter eggs were becoming the norm, but they still shared shelf space with other tasty ovals made of toffee, nougat and marzipan. The hollow eggs often contained little novelty nick-nacks, like jokes and spinning tops, or they might be filled with sweets, such as the jelly-coated fruits which were very popular.

During the great sweetshop smash'n'grab of 1916, most of the sweets, toffees and chocolates carried away had been shipped into the second city of Empire from Britain.

As for ice cream, that barely featured outside of some sixty Italian vendors whose sales turf was defined by the length of time it took for their produce to melt. However, by the time, sixteen years later, that the infant Irish Free State was sprucing itself up for the party summer of 1932, the picture was very different.

SWEET MEMORIES
GERALD BLANCHE, THE 1920s AND 1930s

My memories are of Dublin in the 1920s and 1930s. We lived on Lower Baggot Street, in what is now Dublin 2. There were a number of sweetshops in our neighbourhood, but we did not hesitate to wander further afield to get our favourite sweets, going wherever we could get good value for our money. We youngsters were welcomed as if we were millionaires, even though we may not have had more than a few pennies to spend. I never met with any discourtesy from a shop-keeper. They even allowed us to eat our sweets on the premises if the weather was wet or cold. Sweetshops were places of refuge for hungry children. It almost broke our hearts to pass by without entering.

My favourite sweets were Peggy's legs, Whipped Cream Walnuts, Farthing Rocks, bull's eyes, lemon drops, butterscotch, Liquorice Allsorts and Peppermint Mints.

Chocolate was more expensive, but I loved Half-Time Jimmy bars (made by Urney's of Tallaght) which were big slabs of milk chocolate, enough to share around with friends during the interval at a rugby or football match.

I bought most of my sweets in the following shops:

The Dainty Dairy, in Pembroke Street, where all the items were displayed on a shelf in large glass jars, and were either counted singly or weighed, depending on how much money you had to spend.

Lemon's on O'Connell Street, who stocked the largest selection of boiled sweets in Dublin.

Noblett's on Grafton Street, whose window displays of sweets were always an enticement to us youngsters.

If we were accompanied by an adult or a rich aunt, we might go to a shop called Chez Nous on Lower Baggot

Street, just down the road from our house, where so-called high-class sweets were sold.

It was not every day I could afford to buy sweets. I got my pocket money every Monday morning, sixpence or a shilling, according to my age, and this was supposed to last for the week. On birthdays, you could break out and buy almost anything, with maybe ten shillings to spend. Holiday time was also an exception. Whoever accompanied us to the sea for a swim often brought a bag of sweets, giving us one or two after a swim to take away the taste of salt water.

We also made our own sweets and chocolates at home, which were excellent in quality. However, they lacked the excitement and ritual of actually buying sweets. This latter transaction was a very important lesson for children, teaching them to get value for money. It was also an occasion when we could assert our independence and follow our own whims.

Like most Catholics, we gave up sweets for Lent each year. I was at a boarding school where we didn't get our Easter holidays until Easter Saturday morning. Lent ended at 12 noon on Easter Saturday. Set free, we travelled by train to Dublin. As soon as we reached the big city about 1 p.m., there was a mad rush to buy sweets at Lemon's of O'Connell Street.

Oh, for the simple joys of life!

We All Scream For Ice Cream

At the start of the 1930s, ice cream remained a rare and expensive luxury, and its manufacture was dominated by a handful of Italian immigrants working from what were little more than modified kitchens. But ice cream was on the cusp of becoming big business. People loved it and were willing to pay a premium price. Large dairies began to see the potential for a new spin-off with high profit margins, and the trade was about to put on a spectacular spurt.

Returning from a London industries fair in 1928, which had showcased new ice cream machinery, one writer noted how: 'All classes of men and women were buying and eating ice cream, enjoying it and asking for more.'

He continued: 'Undoubtedly the ice cream trade is going to enjoy a greater popularity this year than it ever did before, and confectioners would be well advised to make special efforts in catering for this business.'

The eating of sweets was still seasonal. Chocolate and cough drops were regarded as a safeguard against the chills of winter, while ice cream was the high point of long, hot summer days.

The writer protested that Ireland was ill-prepared for the Next Big Thing, tourism. In neighbouring Britain: 'Easter generally brings us to the beginning of fine weather and people begin to spend more time out of doors; motoring and cycling are responsible for tempting folks into the country for short trips, but in many directions there is no attempt made towards catering for the refreshment requirements of these tourists.

'On one hand, there is the local hotel, with its heavy unsuitable meals and high charges, and on the other, third-rate tearooms, where minerals are served in pint tumblers half-an-inch thick, and teas in gruesome cups.

'In every district of a large city and in the main street of every county town is a leading confectioner; or there is a confectioner who can be the leader if he or she tries. Trippers want light, inexpensive refreshments, and we believe that ices will be the popular call this season. The confectioner who studies this trade and sets out to cater for it will reap good profits. Ingredients and utensils must be of the best, for it is better to have the name of supplying the dearest and best confections as the cheapest and worst. A good recipe should be obtained, and, if satisfactory, it must be rigidly adhered to year in and year out.

'The ice cream trade is a profitable one, and the prospects of it are worth investigation.'

And investigating those prospects was precisely what more and more proprietors were doing.

As the writer noted: 'The departure of this trade from the legitimate ice cream shop is one of the remarkable features of present-day conditions, the majority of sales being transacted in cafés, confectionery shops and by outdoor vendors. The old-time ice cream shop is being gradually pushed aside, and, in due course, must vanish altogether.

'Perhaps the reason is not far to seek. The present generation of youth is not like its cast-iron forbears, who took pleasure seriously – revelled in plate-glass mirrors, marble slab tables, box-like compartments, where they sat cooped up out of sight in an atmosphere as chilly as the ice cream itself. The youth of today wants to be seen and admired, and chooses the café where everything is open to the view, where they sit at round tables in wicker chairs and emulate screen society modes and manners.

'They want music, even a gramophone.

'Antonio's saloon, gilded and glittering, which we patronised in the days of our youth, looks sad and woebegone today, for it hasn't changed a bit. Youth has, however, but Antonio has failed to see it.

'The trade is going elsewhere.'

PRE-1930S
TOP 10 SWEETS

1 SUGAR PLUMS

A type of dragée sweet made of dried fruits with a sugary coating. Sugar Plums weren't necessarily made of plums – the centres might be of dried apricots, cherries, dates or other fruits.

2 LIQUORICE ALLSORTS

Imported from Britain by Bassetts. The Sheffield firm had made liquorice sandwiches since the 1840s. Allsorts were created when a sales rep dropped the tray of samples, mixing them. His client asked for the muddled selection and Allsorts were launched in 1899, though the Bertie Bassett mascot wasn't unveiled until 1929.

3 SILVERMINTS

Created by Irish firm Clarendon Confectionery in the 1920s. Silvermints were always a steady seller; the melt-in-your-mouth mints soared in popularity during the 1970s on the back of a television ad campaign featuring the cool, clean hero, Steve Silvermint.

4 JELLY BABIES

Jelly Babies, or Unclaimed Babies as they were initially named, were born in Fryer's factory in Lancashire in 1864. They were then mass-marketed by Bassetts in 1918 as Peace Babies to mark the end of the First World War before being finally rebranded as Jelly Babies in 1953.

5 MILKY WAY
Created in 1923 by the American Frank Mars, this bar was named after a milkshake not a galaxy and was the first mass-marketed filled chocolate bar. A lighter version appeared in Irish shops in 1935 touted as 'the sweet you can eat between meals'.

6 WINE GUMS
The first wine gums were created by mixing fermented wine with a gelling agent. Then, in 1909, Charles Gordon Maynard came up with a non-alcoholic version, although he had some difficulty persuading his teetotal father that they weren't promoting drink.

7 TURKISH DELIGHT
Early in the twentieth century, Ireland's best sweetshops stocked Hadji Bey Turkish Delight, produced in Cork by the Batmasian family who had fled troubled Armenia a few years earlier. It was first displayed at Cork's Great Exhibition of 1903–1904.

8 FRY'S CHOCOLATE CREAM
Created in 1866 by the Fry family of Bristol, this was one of the first chocolate bars to be marketed, and also one of the first filled bars. So perfectly conceived it has barely changed in almost 150 years.

9 CADBURY'S DAIRY MILK
Created in 1905 to contain a higher milk content than any previous chocolate, it was the bestseller in Ireland and Britain by the start of the First World War. The 'glass and a half' of milk slogan came in 1928.

10 SHERBET FOUNTAIN
Recipes for fizzy sherbet powder go back to the 1860s and it's possible that the first powders were designed to be added to water to make a sparkling drink. The first tubes of sherbet with a liquorice pipe sticking out arrived in Ireland in 1925.

CHAPTER TWO

1930S
MR CANDYMAN,
MISS CLARNICO,
THE BB BOYS AND THE
KERRY MAIDS

In 1977, HB Ice Cream launched a number of new lines, one of which was called 'The Little Devil'. It proved a good name, and went on to become a monster hit but what was unusual about it was that it harked way back to the days before the marketing men got their hands on our sweets.

The Little Devil was the family nickname for a four-year-old boy called Charlie, the mischievous son of one of HB's executives. In the early part of the twentieth century sweets were often given names on such whims, but by the start of the 1930s the big confectionery companies were beginning to take over from the patchwork of smaller local and national firms. The world of sweets began to go corporate.

'Advertising', 'marketing' and 'branding' were the buzzwords of the big companies, and the 1930s saw the creation of brands that grabbed a large market share and that remain brand leaders to the present day. In a burst of dazzling creativity from 1933 to 1939, Rowntree came up in short order with Black Magic, Kit-Kat, Aero, Dairy Box, Smarties and Rolos.

Mars Incorporated produced its first Mars bar in Britain in 1932. The Mars bar was a so-called combination bar, which added a chewy core to the standard chunk of chocolate. Combination bars, which had originated in the United States, were considered low-rent and faddish by established chocolate makers on this side of the Atlantic, but the huge success of the Mars bar turned that snobbery to envy. Mars followed up with another hugely successful combination bar, Milky Way, in 1935, followed by Maltesers, which were marketed as 'energy balls' and aimed at slimming women.

Meanwhile, in Ireland, things were taking their own course during the 1930s. In the decade following independence in 1922, the British sweets manufacturers had continued to dominate the Irish market with direct imports. This situation changed dramatically in 1932 with the arrival in power of the first Fianna Fáil government led by Eamon de Valera.

De Valera had swept to power on the promise of unstitching the economic deal with Britain that was part of the independence package. As a result, an economic war broke out, with Britain boycotting Irish goods and Dev pushing native industry on a self-sufficiency drive.

As part of that drive, tariff barriers were erected to keep out foreign goods by making them too expensive for Irish pockets. To this end, the government slapped a heavy twopence tax on cartons of imported sweets, which themselves only cost twopence in the first place. This doubling of prices encouraged new Irish sweet makers to set up business, and it persuaded British companies, like Fry's and Cadbury's, to set up independent Irish arms of their operations.

When Cadbury's launched its Irish manufacturing operation in 1932 with a hefty £10,000 borrowed from its parent firm in Bourneville, outside Birmingham, one objector on the Cadbury board groaned that the money 'might as well have been thrown into the River Liffey'. Time would show otherwise, as Cadbury grew to become the country's major chocolate player, a position it still holds today.

As Cadbury Ireland's chairman Donal Byrne explained: 'There is a global rule in chocolate that the first one into a marketplace establishes the taste and texture DNA for a region that all the others who come later try to copy.'

On continental Europe, it was the Swiss firm Lindt

2ᴰ

MILK BAR

CADBURY'S
DAIRY MILK
DIVIDED BAR 2ᵈ

CADBURY'S
FAMOUS
CHOCOLATE
IN A NEW
SHAPE

that had come up with a new super-smooth, super-fine chocolate in 1879 called 'chocolat fondant', which still sets the standard today. In the United States, it was Hershey, though the product they developed was too chalky and gritty for European tastes. Cadbury's in Ireland made a unique blend that was aptly mid-Atlantic in taste and texture. Sweeter than its continental cousins to the east and west, it was, at the same time, richer and creamier than its English counterpart going by the same name. By setting the pace in Ireland early on, Cadbury's also set the nation's taste.

As it turned out, 1932 was to prove a blockbuster year for sales of Irish sweets and ice cream.

The annual Dublin Civic Week was always a bumper time for confectionery sales.

Urging his colleagues to make the most of the

festival, one trader wrote: 'It should be quite feasible to turn Dublin Civic Week into Candy Week. Dublin will supply the bands, the fireworks, military and historical displays, banners and streamers. All we need is our own confectionery sections in the procession, our own pretty lady pamphleteers – our Kerry Maids, Willwood Girls, BB Boys, Miss Clarnicos . . . and not forgetting a troop of Mr Candymen – the connecting link between the shops and the show.'

When Civic Week arrived, one report of 'a harvest' for sweet sellers told how: 'Excursion trains are bringing visitors from all parts of the country. Window displays are of a high standard and the judges, on whom the task of deciding the prize cup winners devolves, will have a hard job to discriminate.'

A pageant of Irish industry featured the costumed marchers of Irish sweets manufacturers, such as the blue-uniformed representatives of Blue Badge Toffee Ltd, better known as the BB Boys. These parades were considered a vital visual contact point with the customer.

'About 350 vehicles took part in the procession which was fifty minutes in passing a given point at quick pace. The general public in thousands stood along the route in the rain, and the windows of business and private houses were packed as for some very attractive street spectacle.'

That same summer the third (and last) Tailteann Games came to Dublin. Conceived as an ancient Celtic version of the modern Olympic Games, the Tailteann Games were billed as 'a feast of manly competition' in such areas as gymnastics, Gaelic football, hurling, chess, archery, handball and poetry.

A window-dressing competition staged to tie in with the games was won by Dublin's most celebrated sweetshop, Noblett's of Grafton Street. One writer said: 'The variety and quality of the Irish-made goods displayed are quite an eye-opener to the public, who, for eleven months of the year, never saw one half of the goods featured this week.'

The crowds who descended on Croke Park and the Phoenix Park for the events were said to have given Dublin 'a continental air' and certainly gave a shot in the arm to the newest branch of the confectionery business, ice cream.

However, in terms of boosting ice cream sales, there was nothing in that entire decade to match the effect of the 1932 Eucharistic Congress, which was the making of one young company called HB Ice Cream.

If the Tailteann Games was a largely unsuccessful attempt to stage an Irish Olympic Games, the holding of the Eucharistic Congress was a runaway success as the young state hosted the Catholic world's equivalent to its own godly Olympics.

The bash was a religious orgy of biblical proportions. Churches stayed open all night serving communion to endless shuffling lines of devotees. The influx of Catholic holy men from around the world gave the city what passed for a clerical freak show. Crowds stared at the Sioux priest with his feather headdress and the exotic Indian Bishop of Kottayam. The dusky Archbishop of Galilee cut a striking figure for the locals with his flowing white beard.

Other jolly sights included a troop of Dutch Catholic Girl Guides greeting the Cardinal Legate with a fascist salute. The congress ended with a million of the faithful marching to O'Connell Street for a final Benediction. The march had a strict pecking order. Led by a vanguard of 60,000 men, it incorporated 'cardinals, archbishops, bishops . . . judges, foreign ministers . . . National University representatives'.

And, bringing up the rear . . . 'women'.

The event ran over five days in the warmth of June and from the grandest cardinal to the last footsore woman, they were all mad for ice cream.

The change to the production of ice cream to a much larger scale (from the handful of Italians who had dominated the industry) came about as bigger dairies grew up, recruiting large numbers of dairy farmers to supply milk for bottling. The supply of milk was seasonal, and during a good summer, the dairy farmers supplied a surplus to that needed by households. Enterprising producers saw the opportunity to turn this surplus into ice cream.

Shortly after entering the ice cream business, Hughes Brothers (HB) Dairy of Rathfarnham in south Dublin landed the lucrative contract to supply milk and ice

cream for the Eucharistic Congress. Monasteries, convents, parish houses, schools and other Catholic-owned buildings had been turned into hotels for the tidal wave of visitors, and Hughes Brothers made doorstep deliveries to the lot of them.

HB never looked back.

SWEET MEMORIES
MARTIN CORLESS, THE 1930s

My earliest memories of buying sweets where I lived in Drumcondra in the 1930s was that the sweets were poured onto weighing scales that seemed huge to us, and then transferred into a cone of newspaper made up by the shopkeeper. Good brown wrapping paper and paper bags were far too good to waste on young kids.

The shopkeeper and the kids were both in on a trick where the shopkeeper would wrap the cone so it was really only a half a cone, with the sweets sitting on top. I think we all knew we were only getting a half-measure because that's all we could afford, but everyone was happy with the deception.

Sweetshop Owners' Enemies List

Sweetshops were big business in the two decades between the creation of the Free State in 1922 and the rationing that came with the advent of the Second World War in 1939.

They owed their high status to the fact that sweets were one of the very few luxuries available in an age when consumer goods were scarce, and were one of the rare treats available to a cash-strapped society that had cut its economic umbilical cord to Mother Britain.

Ireland's sweetshop owners prided themselves on the style and elegance of their elaborate window displays.

They prided themselves on the quality of their chocolates, toffees and sugared sweets. They prided themselves on the social standing of their finer customers, and on their own position as pillars of the retail community.

But before the new Free State was more than a few years old, Ireland's sweetshop owners felt that their whole world was under threat. That threat came in many forms – from new-fangled vending machines to travelling hucksters, to new import barriers, to a smoking craze that was spreading like wildfire.

If everything the sweetshop owners feared and hated most could be boiled down to a single word, that word would be 'competition'.

If the average sweetshop owner of 1930s Ireland drew up an Enemies List, it would feature most or all of the following entries.

1 *Door-to-Door Salesmen*

In the cities, shop owners complained bitterly about 'the menace' of young men and women recruited by dark agents to put on uniforms in the style of cinema ushers and sell sweets and fruit at offices, factories, schools, and in the new suburban estates springing up to replace the crumbling inner-city tenements.

2 *Motorised Hawkers and the New Bus Service*

Country sweetshop owners protested against 'the serious handicap and loss imposed by itinerant traders and hawkers, and by the increased omnibus connection with the city'. There were calls for shopkeepers to run hawkers out of town, and for a gigantic £50 a year tax on the vans used by these travelling salesmen. One rural shopkeeper despaired: 'Cheap stuff is being sold all round the countryside to farmers' houses.'

Another sweetshop owner complained: 'The man in the motor van who drives from door to door in the rural districts selling all classes of commodities is causing no little alarm to merchants and traders in the country.'

These travelling shopkeepers threatened to bring 'bankruptcy for the villages and towns'. For one thing, they were bartering sweets and other goods to farm folk for fresh eggs, with the result that the nation's regular egg producers were being 'left short'.

Sales Gimmicks

Sweet sellers argued that they were against giveaways not out of any selfish motive but because these could hurt the retailers who sold the items that were offered as prizes.

'Another unfair form of trading is the increasing tendency amongst manufacturers of various commodities to endeavour to promote sales by the offer of gifts in exchange of coupons. Surely any commodity ought to be saleable without having to offer prizes to the purchaser. Another point is that the offer of such gifts – be they gramophones or fountain pens – is depriving the retailer of a possible sale of such articles.'

Drapery Shops

Dublin's sweetshop owners were outraged to note: 'Among the most striking displays is the showing of Easter eggs in Messrs Pims' windows in George's Street, Dublin.' The sweet manufacturers were to blame for selling to these unsuitable outlets and the sweetshop owners must give the factories an ultimatum: 'Sell your goods to chemists and drapers, or to confectioners, but you can't sell to all.'

They insisted that only they, confectioners of long standing, had the special skills required to sell sweets to 'a stationary purchasing community'. They argued that: 'To break down the conservative tastes of the people requires persistent salesmanship. There is no short way towards cutting out the established article, and if the confectioner, with all his knowledge of the trade, cannot build up sales for a sweet, how can the draper or the chemist who is catering for the same people?'

Chemists and Head Shops

In the early 1930s one sweet seller complained: 'The chemist is now busily engaged in securing a footing in the sweet trade, after successfully surmounting the difficulties incidental to purveying wine.'

Sweets and alcohol were being sold by so-called 'dairy shops' with names like Hyacinth, Bluebell and Tulips. These were the 'head shops' of their day, selling alcohol outside the normal licensing hours and on 'dry' days, such as St Patrick's Day. Many chemists operated in the same blurry legal area as these dairy shops, much to the annoyance of confectioners and other retailers.

One TD worried about women (but not men) going

to get a prescription filled but whose real purpose was to slip a sly bottle of port into their handbag.

Private Houses

There was virtually no regulation or licensing of the sweets trade in the 1930s, with the result that many enterprising householders simply converted a front room or living room into a makeshift shop. These generally sold the cheapest type of boiled sweets and toffees, and did a roaring trade on Saturdays with children stopping in on their way to the movie matinees. One of Dublin's most popular front-room shops was run by the Cuffe family of Drumcondra who lived next door to the Cat and Cage pub.

Soviet Sweets

The new Soviet Union tried to raise foreign currency by selling sweets on the international market. The notion of stocking godless communist confectionery was beyond Irish retailers, who announced they wouldn't touch them. Their message to the public was: 'We had an opportunity of sampling some Russian Bon Bons, retailed at two shillings per pound, and we say that manufacturers in Ireland need not fear competition as far as quality is concerned . . . They have a very pronounced flavour of hair oil, that cheap brand of hairdressing material sold in the sixpenny stores that smells like a dustbin in a few hours. There is no market here for a preparation of hair oil coated with sugar.'

Advertising

Traditional sweetshop owners disliked, and distrusted heavily, advertised new products such as Mars bars and Maltesers because their profit margins on such items were squeezed to pay for the advertising campaigns.

One reporter noted: 'There is unwarranted prejudice against advertised goods and a tendency in some quarters to keep them under cover, taking them out only when the customer demands them.'

Woolworth's

The chain had arrived from the United States via Britain bringing a competitive philosophy that didn't sit well with a cosy Irish retail trade for whom 'price-cutting' was a rude word. By such strategies as knocking twopence off the price of a pound of Urney's Chocolates, the big store drew the crowds, but as far as Dublin's sweetshop owners were concerned Woolworth's was the unwanted foreign gatecrasher at the family do.

10 *Bankers*

On one occasion, the sweetshop owners of Dublin had to bring one of their members to heel for supplying a bank with sweets which were sold to customers queuing at the bank counter.

11 *Burglars*

In the dirt-poor Irish Free State of the 1930s, there was precious little worth stealing. Along with tobacco, sweets were a favourite target of thieves and, on a daily basis, the newspapers carried reports of sweetshops that had been raided.

A typical case, headlined 'A Midnight Chase', told how Bernard McCluskey, aged twenty, of no fixed address and Peter King, who had 'no business', broke into a premises and stole cigarettes and chocolates. At another stopover on the same spree, they carried away a large haul of chocolates, cakes and Bovril to the value of almost £9.

12 *Their Own Staff*

Sweetshops opened long hours, with the result that shop girls (most staff were young women) could work sixty, seventy or, some claimed, eighty hours per week without overtime. Sweetshops were often the last outlets to close each night, staying open until 10 p.m. or 11 p.m. One sympathetic writer went so far as to claim: 'The life of these young people is described as a human tragedy.' However, owners insisted that these long hours were necessary, saying that they did most of their business between 7 p.m. and 10 p.m.

The shop owners were well represented on local councils, and calls for earlier closing almost always met with rejection. As Dundalk Urban Council voted down

9 p.m. closing on Saturdays, one member remarked: 'We have too much early closing and too many holidays.' Saturday night was the big night out on the town for the young, who streamed to the cinema, the variety theatres and the dance halls. Some trade unions urged their members to boycott sweetshops after 7 p.m. on Saturday nights in an effort to persuade owners to release their assistants, but to no avail.

It took the start of a war for the opening hours to be curbed. In late 1941, in an effort to reduce the power expended on lighting, confectioners and other shops were ordered to close at 8 p.m. Monday to Thursday, 9 p.m. on Fridays and 10 p.m. on Saturdays.

Ice Cream Vendors

As the 1930s progressed, Ireland's sweetshops slowly got into the business of selling ice cream. Once a store had one of the new storage freezers installed, the owner immediately began to take a dim view of the growing army of vendors selling from hand-pushed barrows and from pedal tricycles. A common complaint was that street

vendors would park their barrow or trike just outside a shop selling ice cream, stealing custom from under the owners' awnings.

14 *The Smoking Habit*

Tobacconists and confectionery shops had yet to merge with grocers into what would become known as newsagents, selling newspapers, cigarettes and sweets under one roof. The first move towards this merger came from the tobacconists, who began to stock sweets, much to the annoyance of the specialist sweetshop owners. The First World War had seen an enormous increase in cigarette production to keep the troops in the trenches supplied. After the war's end, the scale of production remained high, with the result that the number of people who smoked shot up across society in general.

Sweet sellers believed, with justification, that every shilling spent on a pack of cigarettes was a shilling no longer being spent on sweets. One reflected: 'Tobacco has affected the appetite of the people. Confectioners are seeking authoritative information as to the cause of reduced sweet consumption, but it is evident that the tobacco manufacturers have captivated the public taste, as discovered by the bakers, and that bread, sweetmeats and other foodstuffs must await a revival of common sense on the part of the public before prosperity to these industries returns.'

15 *Children*

As is the case today, confectioners liked to deal with adult customers who generally knew what they wanted, went for sizeable purchases and often requested home delivery. In the main, they detested youngsters, known as 'juveniles', who generally had little to spend and dawdled before spending it.

Gimmicks and Giveaways

In the first week of 1865, a confectioner on Dublin's Ormond Quay was offering Twelfth Day Cakes for those celebrating the last day of Christmas with a party. The shopkeeper guaranteed that there would be a one-sovereign coin in each batch of 500 cakes.

The tradition of baking rings, coins and thimbles into cakes stretched back at least to the Middle Ages, while the practice of concealing toys, sweets and novelties inside Easter eggs was also an old one.

The added value that these little gimmicks gave to sweets was driven home to a Philadelphia businessman called William Wrigley Junior in the 1890s when he arrived in Chicago and founded a company to sell household goods. Wrigley's first ploy was to offer soap for sale with the inducement of a free gift of baking powder. To his surprise, customers had little interest in the soap, but bought it for the free baking powder.

So Wrigley dropped the soap and began selling the baking powder, this time offering a free gift of chewing gum with each purchase.

And it happened again. Customers bought the baking powder mainly for the free chewing gum.

So Wrigley dropped the baking powder, put all his efforts into hawking chewing gum, and went on to live the American dream.

In the 1920s and 1930s, there was a huge upsurge in gambling and gaming in both Ireland and Britain, which tied in with a new mass enthusiasm for spectator sports, including football, Gaelic games, horse racing and the greyhound track.

When the Irish Hospitals Sweepstakes started up in 1930, it became an instant global smash, and the following year one journal noted: 'Many retailers are now making a feature of weekly draws for sweep tickets. A numbered voucher is handed to each customer. A draw takes place once a week and the result is announced in the window. A Dublin shopkeeper runs a miniature sweep every day with a minimum stake of one shilling, the first prize being fifty shillings. Needless to say, all of these schemes are illegal, but this is a free country as long as one has no political opinions.'

With the country gone competition mad, the Free State's toffee manufacturers tried to outdo each other by holding competitions with ever more extravagant prizes. These competitions tended to fall into two categories. One was to see who could simply collect the most wrappers, while the other was for contestants to guess how many sweets or tokens were contained in a large glass showcase. And, in some cases, contestants had to collect a certain number of wrappers in order to guess how many sweets were in the container.

Devlin & Sons Ltd, trading as the Triumph Toffee Works, was the maker of BB Cream Toffee. Their 'tastefully arranged' display in the window of a store on Dublin's Grafton Street drew crowds, as hungry urchins and well-heeled shoppers alike lost themselves in mental arithmetic. According to one account: 'The floor is strewn with pieces of Blue Badge Toffee. The centre piece is a glass jar containing a large number of silver pellets, and the public is invited to enter a guessing competition. The

SWEET MEMORIES
PHYLLIS AND HARRY PURDUE (MARRIED SINCE 1958), THE 1930s AND 1940s

Phyllis

Honey Bees were my favourite sweets in my childhood. They were little caramels wrapped in paper and you got ten a penny – brilliant value.

I grew up in The Liberties. Sometimes, for a special treat, our dad would take us for a trip to Woolworth's on Grafton Street. That was lovely, really a pleasure, you'd get great bargains there. And, of course, there was the huge sweet section. You got everything – satin pillows, liquorice sticks, liquorice pipes, bull's eyes, aniseed balls . . . There wasn't much money then, it was the same for everyone, so a trip like that was a special treat.

I remember once I got a shilling off my dad because I was having an x-ray. I got twelve little cakes from a bakery on Clanbrassil Street for that. Heaven!

Everyone gave up sweets for Lent. Any sweets you got, you'd save in a little tin box. And, every now and again, you'd open it, take a lick, and put it back in. By the time Lent was over, of course, they'd be a sticky mess. But they still tasted good!

You might get sweets once a week, it wasn't like it is for kids now. In those days, they all came in glass jars — same for biscuits, you bought them loose too. And hygiene wasn't what it is now, hands went into the jars, clean or not. But the strange thing is, there wasn't as much sickness then — you must have had it in your body to fight it. You never heard of as much food poisoning then either.

Mrs Flynn had a little shop down the road from us on Hammond Street. The counter was in the hall. You'd get tea, sugar, everything you needed there. And, of course, sweets. She had a horse and cart too and sold stuff from that.

You'd queue for two to three hours to get into the DeLuxe Cinema on Camden Street. And there were no sweets in the cinemas in those days, you'd bring your own. Hard boilers lasted, which is just as well given how long you'd have to queue to get in!

Harry

When I was a boy growing up on Dorset Street, there were sweetshops on every corner and a penny would do you very well. Cleeves toffee was the best. They sold it in slabs — that would set you back nine pence — but you could buy a half or even a quarter slab for twopence.

A slab of that toffee would keep you going for a month. Though it didn't do my teeth any good!

Down the road from us was the Red Star — it must have been the first supermarket in Ireland — it sold loads of things you couldn't get in other little shops. And a great selection of sweets.

We moved up to Whitehall in the 1940s, and I remember the Lemon's factory at Tolka Bridge, and the sweet smell that hung in the air. They had a shop in O'Connell Street and I remember my sister, who was the eldest, being sent down with limited money to see what she could get. Sweets were a rare enough thing in those days. Sometimes, she'd return with a small Easter egg, which would be raffled in the family. Easter eggs weren't for your average family, a bar of chocolate was what you'd get.

That Lemon's shop was turned into an ice cream parlour later.

Ice cream parlours became very popular when I was around ten or eleven in the 1940s. Later, when I was dating Phyllis, instead of going to the pub after the cinema, you would go to the ice cream parlour, like the Broadway on O'Connell Street. A knickerbocker glory was a special treat. At two shillings it wasn't cheap, but it was worth it. Fruit, ice cream, whipped cream on top. Delicious.

competitor estimating the correct number of pellets in the jar wins a bicycle. Twenty other bicycles are also offered for prizes in connection with BB Toffee.'

While a new bicycle was a handsome prize for the time, the makers of NKM Toffees were not to be outdone. Based in the Dublin suburb of Rathmines, North Kerry Manufacturing ran a 'toffee ballot' open to anyone buying a quarter pound of their product, with the far bigger prizes of £200, £100 and £50, plus £35 in bonuses for participating confectioners.

Lamb Brothers of Inchicore were determined that their Sunny Smile Rich Cream Toffee wouldn't get left behind as the competition heated up, and upped the ante by offering the top prize of a new motor car to the shopaholic who collected the greatest number of Sunny Smile wrappers.

A reporter at 'a unique function' held at Lamb's factory, wrote: 'The occasion was the distribution of prizes offered by the firm for the largest number of wrappers collected by customers of their Sunny Smile Rich Cream Toffee. There was a large attendance of visitors. The prizes, which were very valuable, included a Renault motor car, which was won by Miss Sheila Hughes, 18 Catherine Street, Waterford, a tiny tot of six years. The second prize of a motor cycle went to Miss Ita Ryan of Limerick.'

In keeping with the tone of the times, the prizes were distributed by a priest.

At the time, a new car was a prize worth far more than the average annual salary, but rivals BB Toffee weren't finished yet.

The makers of Blue Badge grabbed the headlines when the following report appeared in newspapers: 'In addition to monthly prizes for the largest collection of wrappers, the Blue Badge Toffee Company offer the huge award of £1,000 or a house, as a prize for the wind-up of their competition. This prize has probably not been exceeded for value by any other Irish firm or manufacturer.'

Toffee in the 1930s was big business indeed.

At the End of the Day . . .

Facing into an uncertain future, one confectioner delivered a message of faint hope to his fellow sweet sellers:

'The old timer had the advantage that he held the field, excepting the grocer perhaps, who gave away sweets to the youngsters occasionally. He hadn't the draper, the stationer, the stores and the chemist all trying to snatch his sales, as is the case today. Well, we must grin and bear it a while longer. We must concentrate on attractive displays and a tempting variety. The good old public still believes in buying from people who know something about the goods they sell. People like to meet Mr, Mrs or Miss instead of the mysterious being in the background known as 'Ltd', who says 'A Merry Christmas' or 'Thank You' on the back of a sales docket instead of smiling pleasantly at the customer as the goods are parcelled up.'

ভ ভ ভ ভ

1930s Assortment

A Week's Supply of Sweets for Threepence
An Irish sweet seller returning from a London confectionery exhibition at the start of the 1930s declared that there had never been a better time to be a child with a sweet tooth. He wrote: 'For threepence a youngster can get enough sweets to last a week.

'Here is the list: One yard of liquorice tubing, one farthing; dib-dab, one halfpenny; 80 assorted pills, one penny; 40 aniseed balls (which change colour and can be sucked for an hour), one penny.

'The liquorice tubes or telephone lines have, it appears, a number of uses. They can be put under the tablecloth at teatime and, when blown through, a plate can be made to jump across the table. And peas can be shot through liquorice pea-shooters just as well as with tin ones.' (A dib-dab was a pack of sherbet with a lollipop for dipping.)

Sweets For All
As the 1930s began, *The Irish Times* noted that sweets were swiftly becoming a daily indulgence rather than an occasional treat. Under the headline 'Our Sweet Tooth' it reported:

'One of the most surprising features of modern Irish life is the remarkable increase in the number of sweetshops, all of which appear to be doing a very thriving trade. Dublin is particularly well supplied with confectioners' establishments.

'I am told that in provincial towns and rural villages the consumption of sweets is enormous. On fair days, when all the country people throng the streets, it is not unusual for some of the shopkeepers to sell over a hundredweight of sweets.

'It is only in recent years that Irish people have developed a sweet tooth. In pre-war days they had very simple tastes as regards sweets. Country folk, for instance, were quite content with a couple of pence worth of lozenges, bull's eyes and a hard sweet known as Peggy's leg. Nowadays, however, they demand the best mixed sweets, for which they cheerfully pay prices ranging from two to four shillings per pound.'

Travelling confectionery salesmen only had eyes for sweets as they passed through rural towns and villages. One noted: 'Roscrea is a town where a salesman could help to dress a good window to his firm's advantage. The same might be said of Mountrath. Mr Condon has built a nice shop at the Fox & Geese, Naas Road, where the bus stops. One of his windows is devoted to sweets and tobacco and the other to groceries. A display is made of Urney goods.'

For most country folk, one of the highlights of any visit to the capital was the extravagant window displays of the sweetshops clustered on Baggot Street, Nassau Street, Henry Street and, especially, Grafton Street.

The lavish display of BB Toffees in the window of the Dublin Industrial Development Association at the top of Grafton Street was judged to be '. . . tastefully arranged in their familiar colour scheme of orange and blue. The floor is strewn with pieces of Blue Badge Toffee. The centre piece is a glass jar.'

Starting at the BB Toffees window at St Stephen's Green, and strolling down Grafton Street towards Trinity College: 'One finds an abundance of well-appointed establishments almost in a group, each having its own exclusiveness and each maintaining its own particular attractiveness. The Grafton has a wonderful display of high-grade confections, which includes almost every well-known name on the market. Tastefully placed in a variety of positions, throughout the whole scheme one can at once discern such names as Clarnico, Urney, Barker & Dobson, Mackintosh and Fry's.'

Running parallel to Grafton Street, Nassau Street also had its colony of high-class sweetshops of which the most famous was The Bee Hive, which stocked its own customised sweets as well as Urney, Clarnico, Savoy and Cadbury's. One passer-by noted: 'The general tone of the window is, indeed, excellent, as it is very well balanced in the quality of material and colour.'

In nearby Wexford Street, a new store called The Little Toffee Shop had just opened its doors. 'It is a tiny place, but it announces the fact that all the sweets on sale are made on the premises.'

Just across O'Connell Bridge, local manufacturers Lemon's 'have given over their entire window to their own lines of confections. They have some very attractive containers on display and, on the whole, while not elaborate, is very artistic.'

At the start of the 1930s the London food giants Lyons opened one of their Maison Lyons corner houses (food halls) on Baggot Street which featured 'a fine soda fountain' and an extravagant window display of confectionery.

Pointing out that the new addition brought the number

of sweetshops on Baggot Street to nine, the sweet sellers' journal remarked: 'It is doubtful if the latest addition will be hailed with delight.'

All of this fresh competition from new sweetshops and from other stores jumping on the confectionery bandwagon put pressure on the city's confectioners to lower their prices. Some of that pressure came directly from the customers who asked Shopkeeper A why his sweets were more pricy than those of Shopkeeper B. One wrote: 'The retail shopkeeper is on the defensive. He is accused of being a profiteer, an exploiter of the public. There are too many retailers. Some of them will have to go. Prices will have to be controlled. Shops will have to be licensed.'

The government set up a commission in 1932 to investigate whether there were indeed too many sweetshops. The trade association predicted that it would come to nothing, which is precisely what happened.

Sweets to Disappear from our Shelves

The first Fianna Fáil government came to power in 1932 promising to stick high taxes on British imports in an effort to spur Irish industries into standing on their own feet. Ireland's sweet sellers imported most of their wares from Britain at competitive prices and resented being told that they now had to source their stock from Irish manufacturers at higher prices. The stock coming from Britain was cheap because it was mass-produced in modern factory plants. The manufacture of Irish sweets was a far more hands-on affair, requiring a bigger workforce and a higher payroll. The result was a higher cost to the retailer.

The sweetshop owners called for a delay on the new import taxes to allow for Irish factories to get in new modern machinery, or for the British manufacturers to dodge the new taxes by setting up factories in the Irish Free State.

The sweet sellers threatened that: 'Once existing stocks of imported goods in the country are exhausted, retailers will be left with a very small variety to offer to customers. Supplies of cross-channel confectionery are drawing to a finish and imports will soon cease to be featured in the Irish confectioners' windows.'

The government was not for moving on the new duties, however, and the shop owners grudgingly replaced their British lines with home-produced ones.

One firm quick to step into the breach was North Kerry Manufacturing Co Ltd, which was based in the Dublin suburb of Rathmines. It unveiled a new Nu-Kreem Assortment at four pence per quarter pound.

This new range of colourfully wrapped sweets included NKM Star Chocolate Toffee, Popular Butterscotch, Punch Toffee, Mint Toffee, Hazelnut Toffee and Cinema Toffee.

The Yorkshire toffee company, Mackintosh declared its intention to stay in Ireland by producing souvenir tins of Carnival Assortment 'beautifully printed in colours and featuring famous Irish beauty spots and historic Irish buildings'.

Ireland's sweet sellers had always had an ambivalent attitude towards chewing gum. Some refused to stock it, either on the snobbish grounds that is was cheap and nasty, or on the more pious grounds that it was morally damaging. However, when it suited the shopkeepers,

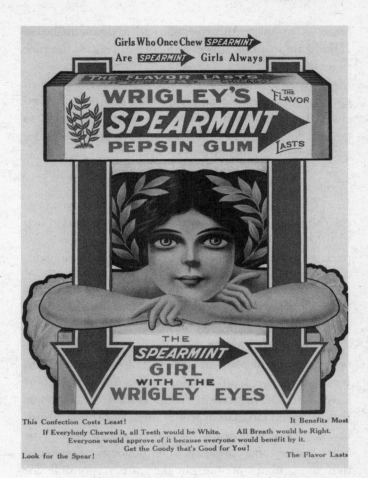

the possible disappearance of chewing gum was used as another stick with which to beat down on the new import duties.

The sweet sellers charged: 'Unless some rearrangement is made, the delectable Wrigley chewing gum will disappear from the Free State, as will other popular brands of this class of sweet. The machinery to make them is so intricate and expensive and the output so large as to make the question of manufacturing in Ireland impossible, unless someone invents a simpler machine.'

Many years later, the country would get its own chewing-gum factory making a brand unique to Ireland called Leaf. In the meantime, the youth continued to go mad for all things American and chewing gum sales grew, despite the higher prices.

Terrorists Strike Cadbury's

In May 1932, the new Fianna Fáil government quadrupled the import duties on sweets, and added belt to braces by slapping on another tax of twopence per package no matter how large or small. For the previous ten years since independence, Cadbury's had continued to import its lines direct from its Bourneville factory in England. Now, however, Cadbury's opened negotiations with Fry's to amalgamate into Fry-Cadbury Ireland.

Cadbury's may have been given an extra push towards opening an Irish plant by armed thugs who demanded Irish sweets for Irish people, as the following report illustrates: 'During recent weeks Dublin confectioners have received circulars warning them not to sell British or foreign sweets, owing to the depressed state of the Free State confectionery industry. The police are convinced that the authors of the circulars are responsible for an incident on the night of May 21st, when four men armed with revolvers and accompanied by three women attempted to set fire to the North Wall, Dublin, premises of Messrs Cadbury Bros Ltd. They stopped several night workers and asked to be shown the exact position of the firm's stores, but they did not gain admission and satisfied themselves with setting fire to a quantity of waste paper against the wall.'

Crazed Kids and Cheap Sweets

For the first three decades of the twentieth century, the business of selling sweets had been a fairly sedate and cosy affair. There had been change, with chocolates and toffees increasingly displacing old favourites like jellied fruits and sugared nuts, but that change had been slow and easy going.

But by the start of the 1930s sweets were becoming cheaper and more available through rival outlets. The old cosy cartel was rattled when the market was suddenly flooded in 1928 with the cheapest candy yet, and the kids couldn't get enough of the stuff.

'Twopence per quarter confectionery has now made its appearance. This is mass production with a vengeance, and two or three Dublin firms are turning it out.

'The system appears to be that only certain retailers in a district are supplied, so that the public makes a beaten track to the privileged shopkeeper, and he scoops up the enormous profits that monopoly always brings.

'Having got to the enviable point of having queues waiting to be served, the retailer weighs it out, parcels it up and earns his profit of say twopence per pound. Naturally, he has to weigh up and sell a great quantity before it becomes worthwhile.

'In the interval, his better class stock is eating its head off, because his customers for the twopence article will be juveniles, and they will pass everything else so long as the craze lasts. The retailer therefore gives himself double the selling task to reap less than the usual margin expected.

'Where is the sense in manufacturing an article of this description? Does it do anybody any good? The loss to the retailer is the worst aspect of all, because of the extra handling and the loss of sales of better quality goods at decent margins of profit.

'All fair-minded traders must condemn competition of this description; just as the lending library has injured the sale of published books enormously, so must sweets for 'next to nothing' injure the whole confectionery industry.'

The writer claimed that the cheap sweets almost certainly originated in England and were 'invented possibly for sale from handcarts in the various market places which are a feature of so many English industrial centres and have no parallel in Ireland. The article cannot do so much damage to the legitimate trade in England as here. When we find Irish retailers selling what was originally intended for barrow sales, and thus undercutting even Mr Woolworth, it is time to warn confectioners that they cannot earn a proper profit on this article unless they can command an enormous sale. This the average confectioner cannot do.'

Sweets for Surgery, Shock and Nerves

Tens of thousands went to bed hungry every night in 1930s Ireland, so as sweets and chocolate bars became more available, they were often marketed as a valuable source of nutrition.

One article entitled 'Sugar Is Good For You', stressed the medicinal benefits of the sweet stuff.

'The great value of sugar, both in the treatment of certain abnormal conditions and in the maintenance of sound health, is comparatively a recent discovery. People are surprised when a doctor recommends sugar in large quantities in the diet of a child. Nowadays, there are other frequent occasions when we make use of the virtues of sugar in the treatment of the young.

'One of these is in connection with operations and the taking of anaesthetics. It has been found that to feed the child with an extra amount of sugar for the day or two days preceding operation is a safeguard against certain dangerous symptoms to which children are liable after taking anaesthetics. Sugar on these occasions is used not only as a preventative, but also after operation as a cure should severe sickness or shock ensue.'

Another feature, entitled 'Heart Food Vs Poison', recognised the growing battle between sweets and cigarettes for the scant disposable income of the Irish public.

It urged: 'Let us eat more sweets. Delicious chocolates filled with many-flavoured fondants, with pistachio, with jam and raisins, with liqueur and with nut, with a hundred intriguing centres inside their soft brown coats. Marrons [Italian glaces] with a tender subtle taste and a

delicate ambrosia of sugar coating. Caramels that yield lingering sustenance in delicious flavours of chocolate, coffee or just caramel before they pass into liquid nothingness. Dragées [decorative sweets] that yield a delicious almond from a tasty succulence. Fruit comfits that bring back memories of orchards laden with fruit.

'Why must they be forsworn? The lollipop was childhood's first joy. Crumbling brown rock affectionately called peg's leg; peppermint and clove sugar sticks; chocolate in pieces of four squares; butterscotch that could be sucked for hours before the final parting in a crunching bite. All these are among the happy memories of a childhood which demanded its energy food in sweets as nature taught it.

'It is not natural to refuse sweets. Sugar is heart food as tobacco is heart poison.

'A pretty woman munching a chocolate is a far more attractive sight than an equally pretty woman smoking a cigarette. It is a more natural sight. Far be it from me to decry smoking, but sweet eating is a natural habit and smoking an acquired one. The earliest craving is for something sweet. Babies know it, and gurgle into happiness when something sweet is put between their rosy lips. Eating sweets makes one feel young, whereas smoking makes one feel more mature. To keep young and to look young one should consume a certain amount of sweet stuffs.

'Mothers and aunts, grandmothers and grandaunts lived to a healthy happy old age without putting on more weight than made for comely rounded beauty. They lived without 'nerves' because they ate as many sweets as they liked.'

Liquid Sweets for an Underage Girl

In the eyes of the law, a great deal of the drink sold as wine in the Ireland of the 1930s was not wine, but sweets. This emerged when Patrick Flynn, a chemist of Parnell Square in Dublin, was fined forty shillings for selling wine during prohibited hours on a Sunday to an underage girl. He was fined a further forty shillings for having the bottles exposed for sale.

Imposing the penalties, Justice Little pointed out that the law defined 'wine' as an alcoholic drink made from grapes and imported into Britain and Ireland. But, according to the judge: 'In truth and in fact [most of it] has been manufactured in this country from a mixture of fruit, sugar and other materials and is subjected to a process of fermentation. This is not wine at all. The proper description of liquor so produced is, according to the Act, an astonishing one. It is provided that such a mixture should be labelled "sweets" and may only be sold as labelled.'

Unfortunately for the chemist, the substance he'd sold illegally was in fact real imported wine made from grapes, so the fines stood.

People Eat Sweets at Bullfights

By the dawn of the 1930s, the popularity of staged sporting events was soaring to heights never before witnessed. Huge crowds surged to football matches, GAA fixtures, horse races and other events, and confectioners jumped on the bandwagon. Urney's produced their Half-Time Jimmy with a design showing a footballer jogging to the pavilion for his half-time refreshment. Packed in bright cartons, the bars came in six flavours including coffee, vanilla, and fruit and nut. According to the blurb: 'The title is calculated to create a big vogue amongst devotees of all sport, and for the nimble sixpence a choice satisfying meal.'

Confectioners who supported motor racing through adverts or sponsorship complained they got a poor return for their money. One wrote:

'The Phoenix Park Motor Races are over, and the guarantors are called upon to pay more than in any previous year. The races are already forgotten, and it is questionable if any good is derived from these displays of speed. Certainly the trade of the city outside of a few hotels does not benefit. In the Isle of Man a young man has lost his life in the TT Trials and the sum of his achievement is nothing.

'Bullfights are less risky and more spectacular. Besides, people eat sweets at bullfights.'

Too Posh for Peanuts

Established sweetshop owners were set in their haughty ways and tended to treat new products with suspicion. Chewing gum, for example, was widely regarded as a bad habit rather than a proper sweet, and many sweetshops refused to stock it. Publicans were less fussy about selling gum, which was often pitched as a 'thirst quencher' to patrons who might not have had the money or inclination to buy a drink. When salted peanuts arrived in Ireland, many confectioners again felt that the product was beneath them, opening a sales window of opportunity for the pubs. According to one report:

'The day of chewing gum as a thirst quencher seems to be over. People no longer require thirst quenchers except perhaps in America, where there is now nothing left to drink [a reference to Prohibition which lasted from 1920 to 1933].

'Mister Wrigley, the chewing gum magnate, is up against it, for the contest seems to lie between chewing gum, the thirst quencher, and salted peanuts, the thirst promoters. These gloomy thoughts are prompted on viewing "Salted Peanuts" in gaily lithographed packets in the public houses. They are only sold by publicans, for the licensed trader has been quick to note the selling possibilities of an article of this description and has taken it to his bosom, so to speak.'

The writer issued a warning to his fellow sweetshop owners, pointing out:

'If the publican finds the attractive little packets going well, it will not be long until he has other attractive packages alongside to keep the peanuts company. We will find by and by that when his customer has eaten so many salted peanuts that he cannot walk in a straight line, he will be coaxed into taking home a box of chocolates for his wife.

'The situation is fraught with difficulties for the confectioner, but we do not think it need cause us worry. We have the satisfaction of knowing that with liquor at its present price the man who eats too many salted peanuts will hardly have enough change left to buy chocolates at the bar.

'Besides, whilst the public does not jibe at drapers displaying confectionery, we think there is a rooted objection in most people to buying sweets anywhere else than in a sweetshop.

'This much, however, emerges from the present situation – the salted peanut has driven chewing gum sales back to the sweetshop!'

It's on the Cards

In a time when advertising was in its infancy, the retail trade supported a busy sector of professional signwriters who painted and designed shop fronts. Part of the service provided was the writing of showcards for display alongside the goods on the shelves. The sweet companies distributed their own cards, often featuring a picture of a pretty woman or a country scene, but these additional neatly hand-printed cards drew the customers' attention to new arrivals and special offers.

One expert advised progressive sweetshop owners:

'You should have a showcard writer permanently engaged to write fresh cards for your shop. Keep him busy at least once a week, for that is the number of times you should change the showcards you exhibit to advertise your own business.

'The manufacturers' cards should fit in with your own, and added to them should save you the expense in showcard writing, but they should never altogether take the place of the showcard, written to order, which should be the expression of your shop's own ideals.

'Get them written to advertise your latest idea! Let them familiarise the public with the fact that you have a living trade, and that you want to keep it! Spread them where the public will see them readily! Let them support the goods you expose in the windows! Limit yourself to a dozen fresh cards a week, if you like, but show at least that number, fresh and newly written up, and you will be surprised at the quantity of new business you do. Let them be artistic before all else. There is not the least use writing them out badly and then expecting people to hurt their eyes reading them!'

Remembrance of Sweets Past

Nostalgia for the lost sweets of our childhood is not a modern development of this retro sweets age. Back in the 1930s, one writer pined for the treats of his youth back in the time before chocolate became widely available.

He wrote: 'It is not more than thirty years ago since chocolates swept so many of the old-fashioned sweets out of the confectionery market. There came many other dainties as well. Crystallised fruits had at an earlier time gained new admirers, and the manner in which they were put up was so tempting and artistic that the public held them in high appreciation. Unlike the old sweets, which were sold loose and were spread out on the shop windows without any adornment, the new favourites were so handsome in appearance that it was easy to understand why the mild change, yet revolutionary in its ultimate effect, took place.

'Gone are the pan drops, the peppermint rock, the bull's eyes, the cough drops. Of Turkish delight we hear but seldom, of sugar barley not very often, and horehound is to be reckoned as one of those which have diminished in popularity or are forgotten altogether. [Horehound was a hard-boiled sweet flavoured with the minty horehound plant and often sucked as a cough drop.]

'Like the Valentines, which were one of the heavy burdens on each 14th of February of the smiling postman, our old sources of merriment, the conversation lozenges, have ceased to carry loving sentiments between bashful or diffident young people. In the past,

these conversation lozenges had a great vogue, and the inscriptions were duly read and admired before this not particularly inviting sweet was swallowed, either with delight at the message it had borne, or as a mark of scorn for the individual who had the hardihood to present it to a disdainful young maid.'

The soppy conversation lozenges in question, or conversation hearts, briefly fell out of favour in the 1920s and 1930s when women adopted the free and flouncy clothing of the flapper, taking up smoking and generally asserting a greater degree of independence. However, they have long since made a comeback and are today known to us as Love Hearts.

Another possible reason that these inscribed sweets suffered a dip in popularity was that they were hijacked by the anti-drink Temperance Movement which replaced coy messages such as 'Do You Love Me?' with more strident ones like 'Misery, Sickness And Poverty Are The Effect Of Drunkenness' and 'Take Ye Not To Strong Drink'.

War Against the Machines

The first coin-operated vending machines appeared in London in the early 1880s dispensing postcards. Within a couple of years, the confectionery industry had cottoned on to their sales potential and, in 1888, the first machines appeared on New York train platforms selling chewing gum. Within another decade, the Pulver Manufacturing Company in the US had added small mechanical figures that performed actions when a coin was inserted for gum. These, in turn, eventually gave rise to pinball machines and slot machines.

As with most new ideas, Ireland's sweetshop owners were highly suspicious of these new-fangled gadgets. Promoters of the machines claimed that they would allow the shopkeepers to make money even when their doors were closed, but many confectioners feared that rival retailers, such as drapers and tobacconists, would install them and steal the confectioners' rightful trade.

One sales blurb for the new machines read: 'The Pascall Automatic Machine is the latest addition to the penny-in-the-slot machines which are to be seen everywhere nowadays. Fixed outside a shop door, it encourages casual sales, especially after closing time. The machine is entirely automatic, solidly constructed and pleasing of shape and colour. There is nothing to get out of order and it cannot be tampered with foreign coins, tin discs, etc. In exchange for a penny it delivers Pascall's Pearl Drops in roll packets, of which it holds three dozen.'

In fact, as vending machines gained in popularity, the newspapers began to carry regular court reports of individuals charged with inserting foreign coins, tin discs and other prohibited items, or with simply taking a crowbar to the machines.

Machines located outside shops were also prone to assault by the Irish weather. Under the headline 'Automatic Machines Losing Ground', one report said: 'The severe weather of the past few months has played havoc with the contents of automatic vending machines, to the loss of the retailer, whilst the machines themselves are losing their freshness. Numbers of retailers who bought such installations on the hire system are beginning to regret the transaction.'

Sweetshop owners attempted to mount a boycott of the automatic machines, but halting the march of progress proved a task beyond them. According to one writer: 'It was reported that a new brand of automatic machine was to be seen in the neighbourhood of Dundalk from which Beechnut chewing sweets were alleged to be purveyed. It is hoped that the information is incorrect, as it was generally believed that the automatic machine had by consent disappeared from this country.'

The Threat from Woolworth's

By the start of the First World War in 1914, Woolworth's had opened several stores in Ireland, with outlets on Dublin's two busiest shopping strips, Grafton Street and Henry Street. Based on an American model, Woolworth's sold a wide variety of goods from clothes to records to toys to sweets, all at rock-bottom prices.

Sweetshop owners hated Woolworth's, as the stores were able to buy in bulk and undercut the prices of rivals. One report of the Confectioners' Association noted: 'The mention of the word Woolworth at an association meeting brings forth an aggressive attitude from at least 90 per cent of the members present. There is an unwritten law that manufacturers supplying Woolworth's with cheap confectionery do not get orders for better class goods from these members.'

Urney Chocolates based in the Dublin village of Tallaght threw their lot in with the sweetshop owners and refused to supply Woolworth's with their sweets at cut price. But the attempts by the sweetshop owners to bully factories into charging Woolworth's full price proved a failure. The only thing left for the shopkeepers to do was to leave Woolworth's selling the cheap sweets, while the sweetshops carried different lines at higher prices.

By the start of the 1930s, when refrigeration was still a novelty in many parts of the country, Woolworth's had all the equipment necessary to become the biggest sellers of ice cream in Ireland. Queues formed in both of their Dublin stores from morning opening to evening closing to buy their famously creamy cones. Hughes Brothers (HB) won the contract to supply all of Woolworths' ice cream in the late 1920s and the chain remained HB's biggest customer until the late 1960s.

What Women Want

A 1910 advert aimed at men suggested that a nice box of sweets was the ideal device for taming a wayward woman. It advised: 'If he understands women, he will take her to the confectioner's and when she is chock full of candy, she will be a very agreeable young woman.'

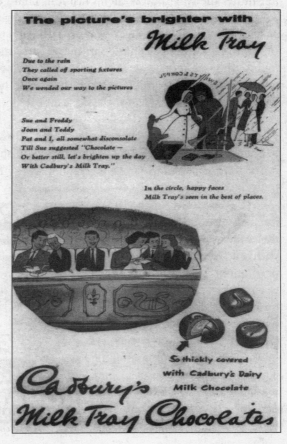

Twenty years later, the advice being given to sweetshop owners was just as sexist, but in a slightly different way. Shopkeepers were urged to cultivate 'the increasing trade which is always in search of novelty in things to eat'.

By this, the writer was referring to women who were hopeless slaves to fashion and novelty. He stated:

'The fact that women form about nine-tenths of a confectioner's customers should be sufficient indication to him of the need for constant change in his stock. If he studies the way that women's fashions change, he will see that there is no creature on the Earth so variable and so capricious in its tastes as woman. With each changing month, she requires a change in her environment, and failing that change, she will create it for herself by purchasing new furniture, new clothes or, if her purse will not extend so far – and even when it does – new sweets and new cookery books.'

Unfortunately for the confectioner, those same women were so fettered to the whims of fashion that every passing new fad could lead them astray from the path to the sweetshop.

At the beginning of the 1930s, the sweetshop owners found themselves in fierce competition with a new hairstyle, the permanent wave. One moaned:

'Young girls who a year ago thought nothing of spending five or six shillings a week on chocolates and other sweets are now spending about a shilling. The rest of their pocket money is going into the coffers of the people who shingle, bob and wave their hair.

'Tens of thousands of the girls in England pay half-a-crown every weekend to have their hair waved. The wave keeps in for about five days. They pay another shilling to have it trimmed and another sixpence to have a neck shave. The hairdressers are also persuading thousands of the English factory girls to have their hair permanently waved! This costs anything from thirty to a hundred shillings!

'If the shingling craze is not so rampant in Ireland at the moment as it is in England, you can rest assured the day is not far distant, and I pass the tip on to fellow retailers in Ireland that it is up to them to see that they retain their hold on the public and go all out to create in their minds the desire to purchase the confectionery they have to offer rather than waste their money on their hair and face.'

And if the young women weren't squandering their spare cash on hairstyles, the modern world put other temptations in their way.

According to the *Evening Herald*: 'It used to be the fashion long ago when girls were girls and never received the attentions of young gallants except in the parlour with the consent of their parents, for the said young gallants to come armed with beribboned boxes of chocolates and to offer them with the time worn remark: "Sweets to the sweet." Nowadays, according to the confectioners and the proprietors of sweetshops, it is the young gallants who have the sweet tooth, and milady prefers a hundred of cigarettes or an invitation to a dance.'

Marzipan Fish and Chips

The onset of the cold, dark days of the Irish autumn were welcomed by sweetshop owners as the start of the chocolate season. When the clocks turned back, one wrote: 'Shop windows seem to take on an added attractiveness, now that they are lit up at about 5 p.m., and passers-by pause to look at the displays. Bright lighting, backed up with choice display, increases the selling chances immediately.'

As the nights drew in, another enthused: 'Confectioners report a general livening up of trade. The chocolate season has commenced. Some good orders have been placed for Christmas novelties. Queues are beginning to form up at the theatres again, dancing is in progress everywhere, so there must be money about.'

The hefty tariffs imposed by the new Fianna Fáil government in 1932 meant that there was a scarcity of imported Christmas novelties that year. The Sweet Sellers' Association called on Irish firms to take up the slack and get into the business of 'fancy box making'.

But even as the trade body was urging native firms to tool up for new packaging opportunities, it was reporting that the end was nigh for sweets in tin cans and the traditional big glass jars.

The association reported: 'The tin canister industry, as well as the bottle industry, is likely to receive a nasty knock in the near future when the new pulp containers make their appearance. The idea is an American invention by which the paper pulp, on being mixed with certain chemicals, is blown into a mould on the lines of glass bottle blowing. All shapes can be moulded, from bottles down to packing cases, without joinings of any kind. They are rigid, stand a pressure up to 100 pounds, are waterproof, odourless and tasteless, and cost little to make.'

Despite the price hikes imposed by the 1932 government, the British firm Maynards persuaded some Irish retailers to stock their Christmas novelties which, the makers promised, 'make excellent window displays'.

These included: 'The Original Lucky Snowman. Chock-full of mysterious numbered parcels containing assorted toys. Variously priced at one shilling, one and six, or three shillings.

'Smokers' Outfits. The ever-popular smokers' cabinets 'just like Daddy's' containing chocolate cigars, cigarettes, matches, etc.

'Penny Chocolate Christmas Tree Decorations. The entire factory output for many months to come is already sold.

'Jack Tar Smokers. [Jack Tar was a nickname for British sailors.]

'Snowballs. Invaluable at parties. When opened, disclose unexpected gifts.

'Marzipan Fruits. Extensive range and various fancy packing.

'Marzipan Fish and Chips.

'Marzipan Pastries.'

While chocolate was successfully pitched as a nutritional snack to keep out the winter chill, by the 1930s, toffee was cornering a growing share of the same market.

One confectioner wrote: 'Peppermint is always largely consumed as a flavour during the winter months, and toffee flavour with it was taken into favour some years ago. Somehow the unique combination of so many good things – milk, butter, sugar – by an ingenious process, has taken hold of the public taste so that it will not willingly dispense with its toffee during the winter months. There is this to be said for both toffee and chocolate, and perhaps most of all for toffee, that in this northern climate they both have a distinctively warming effect upon the human circulation, and seem to make the cold air itself more intense. They are both largely nourishing.'

Sweaty Windows and How to Fool the Customer

One of the big problems facing sweetshop owners in the 1930s was the curse of sweaty windows. The whole concept of mounting a window display involved putting the best, most attractive and most expensive items on show. To keep out flies and other intruders, the displays were boarded up from behind with a fetching backdrop.

However, as a result of this sealing-in process, there was virtually no air circulation, which meant that the sweets warmed up in the sunlight and then chilled in the cold night. This resulted in sweaty windows, which were hard to see through, and weather-worn sweets.

When the weather outside turned hot, confectioners removed the bulk of their display sweets to a more friendly in-store climate, but this left their prized display looking a mite threadbare.

Happily, help was at hand.

It was reported: 'The amount lost annually by confectioners through chocolates sweating in window displays must run to very large sums and retailers will be glad to know of a new idea . . .. This innovation consists of dummy chocolates of every shape and form, which are faithful reproductions of the original chocolates. The firm [manufacturing the dummies] undertakes to copy faithfully any brand of chocolates in regard to shape, colour and piping, at very moderate prices. If makers generally adopt the idea of dummies for window display, the saving to the retailer will be immense.'

But even when the sweaty window displays were tackled, there remained the problem of sweets that just wouldn't sell, known in the trade as 'shelf-stickers'. The answer, suggested one writer, was to pull a fast one on the customer. He wrote:

'The first thing that should be noted is that the public have – fortunately for us in this respect – very short memories. It is possible to call a confection by an entirely new name, and change the name again inside a week, and the public will know no difference! They will believe it is a new line.'

The advice to sweet sellers was that if you just leave shelf-stickers sitting there in full view, they will stay stuck. Instead, he counselled:

'By far the best thing is to take the whole lot away and put them out of sight for a time. You must clear your counter of them as well as the window, and feature in your window and counter display only the lines that will go. Aim at instilling into the minds of the public that you have got rid of the slow sellers.

'At the end of the month get busy on them. Go about your task of shifting them in whole-hearted fashion. If you have a dozen boxes of wrapped caramels or toffees, don't display them in the same box or bowls that they were displayed in before. And at all costs don't forget to call them by a different name. This is not dishonesty, but enterprise.'

The line between enterprise and dishonesty regularly blurred over, as several court reports from the period show.

In one case, Fox Glacier Mints Ltd sued one Bill Cullen for passing off Barker & Dobson's Glace Mints as Fox's Glacier Mints at his shop on Dublin's O'Connell Street. The confectioner admitted that if he ran out of one make of sweets he'd pass off another line under false pretences. At the same court sitting, Fox also successfully sued Woolworth's for passing off Williams & Woods mints 'when Fox's were called for'.

1930S
TOP 10 SWEETS

1 PEGGY'S LEG
Around forever and unique to Ireland, this was a rough and ready toffee combining brown sugar, syrup and molasses, and flavoured with ginger. The goo was pulled into sticks resembling stilts rather than legs.

2 MARS BAR
Created in 1932 by the English arm of Mars Incorporated, this was a sweeter counterpart to the American Milky Way, which was a completely different beast to the feathery Milky Way launched in Ireland in 1935.

3 MALTESERS
Made with barley malt and so slight they're designed to merely tease the palate, Maltesers were created in 1936 by Forrest Mars Senior. They were initially pitched to slimming women as low-fat 'energy balls'. Early slogans included: 'The chocolates with the less fattening centre.'

4 PINT BRICK OF ICE CREAM
An Italian invention of the nineteenth century, the pint brick of ice cream was introduced to Ireland in 1933 by Hughes Brothers. Carried home wrapped in newspaper to keep it refrigerated, the Sunday after-church brick became a status symbol of the rising middle class.

5 KIT-KAT
The four-fingered bar was created after a Rowntree worker suggested making a snack that 'a man could take to work in his pack'. Launched as Rowntree's Chocolate Crisp in 1935 it became Kit-Kat Chocolate Crisp two years later.

6 SMARTIES

In 1937, Rowntree's rebranded their long-running Chocolate Beans as Smarties Chocolate Beans. The original selection featured eight colours each with a different flavour. Following complaints that the word 'beans' was misleading, the name became simply Smarties.

7 BLACK MAGIC

The classy assortment took off in 1933 with a revolutionary advertising campaign which gave the product a back story. As a honeymooning couple gazed out across glistening Venice, a scribbled note in the foreground said: 'Sweet of Alan to think of bringing a fortnight's supply of Black Magic.'

8 CONVERSATION LOZENGES

Dating from the nineteenth century, these were sweets of varying shapes and sizes imprinted with messages ranging from the flirtatious ('Do You Polka?') to the hectoring ('Drink Is The Ruin Of Man'). They have come down to us today as Love Hearts.

9 WOOLWORTH'S ASSORTMENT

There were several Woolworth's stores in Ireland and they infuriated 'proper' sweetshop owners in the 1930s by selling pineapple chunks, rosie apples, mint balls and other boiled sweets at rock-bottom prices.

10 ROLO

Launched by Mackintosh (later Rowntree-Mackintosh) in 1937, these were a simple recipe of Mackintosh's toffee coated with chocolate.

Only One Child Died: The Age of the Rogue Ice Cream Man

In the early decades of the twentieth century, ice cream in Ireland was an expensive luxury manufactured on a small scale by a handful of specialists. During the 1920s a number of dairies spotted the potential to turn surplus milk supplies into ice cream, but early consumers had to take their chances with haphazard hygiene practices, rudimentary pasteurisation processes and a widespread lack of refrigeration which could lead to batches of ice cream melting and being refrozen.

And although the bigger dairies could carelessly lapse into bad habits, some of the backstreet operators were positively feckless about the risk to human health and life.

A contributor to *The Nation* newspaper wrote: 'Ice cream will continue to be suspect until the government take the long overdue step of controlling the making and selling of the stuff. The big manufacturers of ice cream, who use careful methods, are well aware of the damage done to their industry by this extraordinary laxity. At present, there is no legal definition of ice cream. If ice

cream were legally recognised as a food containing a fixed quantity of milk, it could then be inspected like dairy produce and offenders brought to book, to the satisfaction of all honest traders and to the relief of innumerable parents.'

If there was one thing the ice cream sellers hated more than rogue ice cream makers, it was the media getting the general public into a tizzy about rogue ice cream makers.

One member of the Confectioners' Association fumed: 'One of the Dublin evening newspapers favoured its readers early in the month with a lurid "special article" which revealed the "appalling conditions" under which ice cream is prepared in some parts of the city. Some of the investigations disclose a terrible laxity on the part of the Public Health Authorities, which body, on the evidence, should take on to its staff the lively contributor of the article, whose sources of information are unique and worthy of Sexton Blake.

'The article brought the usual flow of correspondence from the usual circle, including one who "manufactured" ice cream in a "caravan", and deplored the conditions apparently existing elsewhere.

'The campaign, however, was brought to a close by a strongly written letter from the Ice Cream Section of the Retailers' Association . . . that their body was aware that manufacture was carried on by unorthodox methods and in doubtful surroundings by a number of people.'

In the summer of 1937, Irish newspapers reported an outbreak of 130 cases of Sonne Dysentery in England over a one-week period. Most of those hospitalised were children who had eaten contaminated ice cream. One 'ice cream car' selling to those picnicking in a field was immediately fingered for poisoning thirty-four people.

The authorities initially suspected that 'at least four itinerant ice cream vendors' were responsible for the 130 cases spread over a wide area of Somerset, but they eventually traced all of the infections down to a single salesman – codenamed Mr H. – who 'showed great reluctance to submit a detailed itinerary of his daily visits'.

When they tracked Mr H. to his DIY factory, they were appalled by what they found. 'It was being made in a lock-up garage. This had a cement floor and galvanised iron sides and roof, but no other conveniences, i.e. no drain, water supply or lighting. The utensils had to be taken home to be washed, and he lived in a back-to-back house which is condemned and waiting to be demolished. The house has a water supply but no means of obtaining hot water other than by heating water on a gas ring or open fire. The cleaning of the utensils is not likely, therefore, to have been very effective.

'The methods of preparation were very simple, the milk being mixed with ice cream powder, sugar and some fresh eggs, put into a metal canister and the contents frozen by standing the container in a mixture of ice and salt. It was frozen in the morning and then taken out on the rounds. Mr H. has a motor van and also a tricycle, while the ice cream was also taken by rail.'

When the health inspectors took a sample of ice cream from the canister they found: 'It was heavily contaminated with B. coli. Two guinea pigs inoculated from sediment both died of malignant oedema within two days.'

All around Ireland, freelance ice cream hawkers were making up their mixtures in similar conditions.

Sweets too were being made in filthy conditions in garages, kitchens and backstreet factories – but mainstream manufacturers couldn't be entirely trusted either. When health inspectors ran a check on seven well-known makes of toffee, all seven turned out to contain cheap and nasty alternatives to their officially listed contents. One of the scientists cited an advert for one line of toffee which claimed it was 'a delightful concord of pure cane sugar, full cream milk and fresh Irish butter – three fine body building foods'. However, tests showed that the toffee contained precious little Irish butter or cream milk. The main ingredient was cheap coconut oil.

But at least an overdose of coconut oil has never been known to kill anyone.

Once in a while, someone died from eating toxic ice cream, and if that wasn't bad enough, retailers resented attempts by the media to inform the public of such occurrences.

When a young child died from poisoned ice cream in the English town of Bath, an editorial in an Irish trade journal blamed the media for damaging business by blowing it out of proportion. It said:

'It is only a couple of months ago since ice cream vendors everywhere were earnestly praying for some decent weather, and now the whole trade is thrown into a state of chaos by the worldwide publicity given to the sad occurrence.

'London ice cream manufacturers have got together and passed a resolution which asked the Ministry of Health to take steps to prevent the broadcast of cases of food poisoning in no way connected with ice cream in such a manner as to create a bias against ice cream.

'Considering that only one child died, we think the press was unjustified in announcing that 200 persons were poisoned. The illness of everybody affected, however, was traced to a germ in the ice cream prepared by one person, and the accident has done the industry an amount of damage from which it will not recover for a very long time.'

Toxic ice cream was not the only threat to life in an age when safety standards were very much an afterthought, if they were thought of at all. The Irish newspapers reported the death of a three-year-old in England who swallowed a novelty balloon.

'A balloon on a short stick of liquorice was produced by the coroner, who described it as the most dangerous thing, and said that these sweets should not be made. Evidence was given that a balloon was found in the child's throat, and after being rushed to hospital the child died of asphyxia. The coroner's office said that he had been to the shop at Sydenham, and the owner had told him that he would not sell any more of these sweets.'

And that was that.

Meanwhile, Italian ice cream sellers in Northern Ireland had an additional set of problems to deal with. The puritanical burghers of Belfast and other towns in the North took a dim view of Sunday trading in any shape or form, and passed a succession of bye-laws restricting opening hours on the Sabbath. The owners of the North's ice cream parlours were largely Catholic and Italian, and the newspapers of the time testify that they came under the constant scrutiny of the law.

After the introduction of yet another new set of opening restrictions, The *Northern Whig* reported: 'The first batch of summonses against ice cream shop proprietors for contravening this regulation were dealt with by the magistrates at the Belfast Summons Court recently, and small fines were imposed. The Italian population of the city was well-represented among the delinquents, and the Clerk of the Court had to have more than one attempt at some of the picturesque foreign names.'

CHAPTER THREE

1940S
A BEASTLY
SHAMELESS BLACK
MARKET IN SWEETS

In the winter of 1943, members of the Advertising Press Club of Ireland sat through a lecture by an American guest speaker entitled 'Advertising With Nothing To Sell'. The sad subject matter neatly summed up the sorry state of a Free State which had been in suspended animation since the rest of Europe had gone to war in September 1939.

Everything was in short supply. Fine Gael's Senator Michael Hayes attacked the Department of Supplies, which he charged had 'given the people a fuel muddle, a tea muddle, a sugar muddle, a petrol muddle, a potato muddle and a situation in which supplies are plentiful only for the rich on the black market'.

Dublin's air-raid shelters were fitted with locked gates because they were being used by the public as toilets and dumps for household waste. The general air of disobedience fostered a crime spree, with the authorities appealing to the citizens of Dublin's inner city to report the removal of banisters, staircases, wall sheetings, doors, floors, lead cisterns and piping from houses. Trees were being illegally cut down and lifebuoys and light bulbs stolen from public places. In the face of this wave of lawbreaking, the best response the Minister for Supplies, Seán Lemass, could manage was to inform the Irish people that they should be happy that they had the most generous sugar ration in Europe.

SWEET MEMORIES
ANNA O'ROURKE, THE 1940s

It was during the war and there weren't a lot of sweets to be had. Even when there were, we didn't have much money to buy them. You wouldn't have them every day. Usually just at the weekend.

I lived in Howth, north of Dublin. Even though it was only a little fishing village it had three sweetshops close to each other. There was Granny Reeves', Malone's and Milligan's, which was run by two Misses Milligan. They had the sweets in lines on the shelves in big jars, including acid drops, aniseed balls, which we called Nancy balls, sweets that looked like playing marbles, satin cushions, Cleeves toffees that came in big slabs, Honey Bee Bars, sweet cigarettes and all kinds of liquorice like shoelaces and pipes.

You could buy four bull's eyes for a penny, but the shopkeepers would sell you a single bull's eye for a farthing. You could also buy just one sweet cigarette if that's all you could afford.

The sweetshops stayed open later than the other shops, so they'd also sell bread and milk for people who'd run out.

Unfortunately, many of the nation's shopkeepers and sweets manufacturers were just as enthusiastic about breaking the law as the general public. The Irish people may have had the most generous sugar ration in Europe, but gouging shopkeepers did their best to see that gullible or easily browbeaten customers didn't always get the modest amount due to them. What sugar they managed to keep from its rightful owner, the shopkeepers sold at hiked-up prices on the black market.

Speaking in the Dáil, Fine Gael's future leader James Dillon deplored '. . . the shopkeeper down the country or in the city who says to poor people when they come in for their weekly ration: "Oh, the ration did not come this

My parents wouldnt allow us to accept money from anyone. We were told to politely say, 'No thank you.' On a special occasion when you were allowed, we had to take it straight home and give it to my mam. If you handed her a shilling, she might give you back a penny to spend in the sweetshop.

The exception was my brother Joe, who'd do some work for my uncle, also Joe. Sometimes, my Uncle Joe would give Joe a half-crown, which was a huge amount of money. Uncle Joe would tell him: 'Don't bring that home to your mam. Run straight off and spend it.' It would be very hard to spend a half-crown on sweets, it was so much. I'm sure Joe must have shared them with the rest of us.

I used to run to the shops to buy snuff for an old neighbour lady. She didn't have sweets, and because I wasn't allowed to take money I got paid with a slice of Vienna roll with butter and jam. Jam was scarce, so it was as good as having sweets.

week. I am sorry. You will have to do without your sugar this week." There are certain innocent types of people who in such cases actually go home without their rations and come in the next week. Then he says to them: "I am glad we have it this week." He then hands out a week's ration to a poor woman and says: "There you are now." The woman knows she has been done out of a week's ration but she does not care to be unpleasant about it. That shopkeeper will subsequently sell that sugar to some poor person who wants it for a sick child at three shillings a pound. If I caught that man, I would give him three years' penal servitude.'

Meanwhile, the confectionery factories were running

a parallel black-market racket, with a lot of product going out the back door instead of to the sweetshops. While some factories supplied back-door spivs, others took advantage of the scarcity by opening their own in-house shop fronts and cutting out the traditional sweetshops. These moves went down badly with the country's confectioners, who ran to their local TDs crying foul.

Former Taoiseach W.T. Cosgrave raised the matter in the Dáil, saying: 'A number of traders have come to me in connection with the distribution of sweets. They have considerable difficulty in getting sufficient sweets from the wholesalers, and, as sweets are not rationed, they have no method of compelling the wholesalers to give them what they consider a fair proportion of their pre-war or earlier years' allowances. Some steps should be taken to ensure that wholesalers are prevented from going into the business of selling sweets as retailers, as a number of these wholesalers have done, or, at any rate, to ensure that, before they do so, sufficient quantities are made available for people whose sole livelihood is the retailing of sweets or who were in business prior to the Emergency.'

Sugar rationing remained in force for some years after the end of the war, and as late as 1947 there was still a thriving black market in illicit sweets.

James Dillon told the Dáil: 'If I could find the person responsible for sending into the streets of the city, women and girls to sell, in flagrant defiance of the law of this country, sweets and chocolates which have been manifestly derived from an illegal source, I think that no punishment would be too severe for him. It is not that I begrudge these poor women and girls the profit they make, but there is some dirty rogue in the background who is sending out these poor people, teaching them contempt and hatred for the law in order to get his own dirty profit. That confectionery which is being diverted from the ordinary trade channels and is being denied to people who have a legitimate claim to it, is being given to others to corrupt them and use them as agents to rob the public. A beastly shameless black market exists in this way.'

Dillon bristled that the suppliers of black-market sweets should be 'ferreted out' and 'ruthlessly dealt with when discovered'. In truth, it wouldn't have taken a Sherlock Holmes to track down the guilty parties, but the political parties had not the slightest interest in tackling a black economy being run by the middle, business and farming classes on whose votes they relied.

ভ   ভ   ভ   ভ

1940s Assortment

People of Northern Ireland Deserve to be Profiteered Upon

Shortly after the start of the Second World War, sugar rationing was introduced in the Free State. Hot on its heels, an Emergency Powers Order was enacted which prohibited the export of a range of products, including 'toys, gongs . . . and sugar confectionery of all kinds'.

While this export ban was easily enforced on the sea routes to the all-important British market, it led to a big increase in sweet smuggling to Northern Ireland which suffered much more severe rationing and shortages than the Free State.

The authorities in the South had an ambivalent view. As an independent TD for the border county of Monaghan, James Dillon suggested that a spot of cross-border give and take was a natural and healthy thing, stating 'there is a lot of tripe talked about the black market'. Speaking of enterprising individuals who in different economic times had transported goods south of the border, he remarked: 'Those people brought in that stuff and paid fancy prices for it and when they got it down here they charged fancy prices for it. I do not think these people were in the black market. I never did, I do not now, and I would never punish them if I caught them.'

The deputy's easy-going attitude seemed to be reflected in the treatment meted out to seventeen local traders who appeared before the Dundalk District Court in 1941 charged with aiding and abetting illegal exports. Specifically, they were charged that at a Sunday market in the town they had been caught selling chocolate, sweets, butter and tomatoes to shoppers from the North, knowing that they were breaking the law.

The case against one sweetshop owner was dismissed when his lawyer argued that the Northern individual who'd bought chocolate from his shop might have eaten it quite legally while still in the South.

The judge warned the remaining defendants that selling sweets in the likelihood that they'd be transported across the border was not only illegal 'but that it is also an immoral offense because it degrades the Lord's Day'. Thirdly, at a time when prices were fixed by government order, the Dundalk traders were guilty of 'scandalous profiteering'. The judge, however, did grant that: 'People coming from Northern Ireland might deserve to be profiteered upon.'

Confirming what everyone already knew, the judge observed: 'The local guards made their reports but nothing was done, and one got the impression that the authorities were winking at the trade, notwithstanding its bad effects from every angle.'

And with that, the judge himself seemed to give a sly wink to the wheeler-dealers. He fined the worst offender five pounds and let the rest of the lawbreakers off with the Probation Act.

A Mass of Black Dough

As the 1930s progressed, sweet making in the United States, Britain and other developed countries became increasingly mechanised. However, most Irish factories were too small and too cash-strapped to invest in the latest equipment, and sweet making here remained very much a hands-on affair, which provided hundreds of low-paid jobs for women.

One factory visitor during the Emergency came away highly impressed, writing: 'Despite the tremendous increase in output and intensive mechanisation, large numbers of sweets are still being made by hand. In any big sweet factory one can still see, not far from an elaborate machine making drops of various hues and flavours at the rate of 6,000 a minute, groups of young girls dipping nuts in bowls of warm toffee, in basically the same way their grandmothers made lollipops.

'In the room next door, row after row of huge three-hundredweight pans whirl on electric shafts putting the sugar coating thinly and evenly on ten tons of almonds and aniseed balls a week.

'Efficient and complicated though modern sweet-making machines are, they are not more impressive than the dexterity of the so-called 'unskilled' girls who make, wrap and bottle sweets by hand at an incredible speed.

'I watched a girl packing peppermints into cellophane wrappers. In less than twenty-five seconds her fingers, flashing along the pastilles, had picked up the exact number, aligned them on a strip of cellophane, rolled it to form a tube, sealed the tube and packed it away in a box.

'To watch a girl conjuring liquorice pipes out of a mass of black dough at the rate of twelve a minute is a fascinating sight. With a few deft movements of her nimble fingers, she grabs a handful of the plastic black mass at her side, rolls it into a carrot shape, pinches the thick end to form the bowl and put the curve on the stem. It is then put with others on a load ready to be taken to the drying chamber.'

Get Ready for the Smoothie

In 1941, with Britain seemingly on the brink of falling to Nazi invasion, the British government banned the export to the Free State of fresh oranges and lemons. Up to a couple of years earlier, hundreds of young boys would gather at Dublin's docks whenever a banana boat docked with thievery on their minds. The Dublin Port and Docks Board were told in 1937 that banana stealing had reached epidemic proportions, that dock foremen tried to chase them away but they just 'scattered' into the surrounding laneways, and it that it was only a matter of time before a fleeing youngster was drowned.

While tropical fruits had all but vanished, Irish readers were encouraged to dream of better times ahead with news from America that the fruit smoothie had been invented and would eventually make its way to Ireland. The report said: 'A new electrical machine, called a Waring Blender, will be installed in cafés, milk bars, etc. It will take a banana and whizz it into a drink for you. The new device was invented by a well-known American band leader Fred Waring. It is priced around £7.'

Something of a smoothie himself, Waring notched up his millionth blender sale in 1954 to add to the millions of records he'd sold and the millions of viewers he was then attracting as one of America's first television stars.

Thinking Outside the Box

With their trade already damaged by factories diverting confectionery onto the black market, the country's sweetshop owners kept up their long-running propaganda attack on the travelling shops which, they complained, 'offer everything from a needle to an anchor', including a range of cut-price sweets.

The rate-paying shopkeepers of Ennis in County Clare believed they had come up with an inventive new plan that would make the problem go away, but they were to be sorely disappointed.

A confectionery journal reported: 'Ennis Urban Council decided to divide, by means of white lines, the market into a number of squares into which [the shopkeepers'] stock could be placed. It was hoped that when stock occupied these spaces on the square, there would be no room for the travelling shop. But the travelling shops arrived on the market day and took up their usual stand. On being asked to move, the owners refused, saying they had been there for years.'

Catholic Ice Cream for a Catholic People

In Britain, one of the earliest casualties of the Second World War was the ice cream trade. Supplies of milk and cream were diverted to making less frivolous foodstuffs, many of the Italians running ice cream parlours were interned as unfriendly aliens, and even Walls' famous fleet of Stop Me And Buy One tricycles were commandeered for use as runarounds on army bases.

In Ireland, the business carried on much as before. The trade war with Britain had ended and, in 1938, exports had resumed, but the wartime disruption to shipping meant that, once again, much of Ireland's dairy produce stayed at home.

Twenty years earlier, Ireland's small band of independent ice cream manufacturers relied on ice shipped from northern climes to make and store their product. As a result, ice cream didn't keep well, couldn't travel far and had to be eaten within a few hours of production.

New electrical freezers and insulated vehicles gave ice cream a slightly longer life and allowed for deliveries farther afield. By the start of the war, the pint brick had become a favourite Sunday treat with those families that could afford it. In fact, as more and more people were moved out of the crumbling inner-city tenements to the new suburbs, having ice cream after Sunday dinner gained a snob-value currency with the new class of upwardly mobile homeowners.

Housewives carried the brick home from the local shop wrapped in newspapers to keep it cool, while shopkeepers carved the bricks into slices which they sold between wafers at twopence a go. In the centre of Dublin, Woolworth's worked with their main suppliers, Hughes Brothers, to develop a special serving knife and a stainless steel marker which pressed onto the ice cream brick dividing it into eleven segments.

Beyond the outskirts of the main cities and towns, the Free State's electricity grid was a scrappy patchwork. Some areas enjoyed a mains supply, others relied on a local generator, while large parts of rural Ireland had no electricity supply at all. The major ice cream manufacturers transported their produce on insulated trucks and by rail, but the narrow pockmarked roads made truck deliveries something of a nightmare. The onset of the Emergency brought severe fuel rationing which restricted road travel and slowed the trains to such a crawl that every consignment of ice cream was in danger of melting.

By the start of the 1940s, Dublin-based Hughes Brothers (HB) had built a supply network to shops on the outskirts of the capital, recruiting retailers who were on the mains electricity grid. HB made a simple offer to suitable stores: the company would supply expensive state-of-the-art fridges imported from the States on condition that the shopkeeper would only use them to stock HB ice cream.

As the war ended, Minister for Supplies Seán Lemass predicted that women would be the drivers of rural electrification, and by extension of ice cream sales across the whole country. The minister predicted: 'The use of electricity in rural areas is going very largely to depend on the attitude towards it of the womenfolk. Although electricity will lessen the burden of farm work upon the males it will be a very special boon to women. I hope to see the day that when a girl gets a proposal from a farmer she will enquire not so much about the number of cows, but rather concerning the electrical appliances that she will require before she gives her consent, including not merely electric light but a water heater, an electric clothes boiler, a vacuum cleaner and even a refrigerator . . . It will make the [marriage] proposition far more attractive to a young lady.'

By the late 1940s, the capital was served by a number of ice cream manufacturers, the biggest of which were Hughes Brothers in Rathfarnham, Merville in Finglas and Lucan Dairies beside the Phoenix Park. If Dublin's autocratic Archbishop John Charles McQuaid was rarely roaring drunk on power, he was seldom sober on it either, and the country's top cleric apparently resented the fact that the ice cream business and most of the capital's milk trade was in the hands of Protestant factory owners. The land-owning Nash family ran Lucan Dairies, the Craigies who owned Merville also hailed from the Ascendancy class while the wealthy Hughes dynasty were also guilty, to employ a phrase of the time, of kicking with the other foot.

According to the HB historians Paul Mulhern and Kieran Fagan, Archbishop McQuaid was a key force behind the launch of Dublin Dairies in 1949, to provide Catholic milk and Catholic ice cream for a Catholic people. Mulhern and Fagan wrote: 'The theory is that Archbishop McQuaid felt it wrong that the retail milk market be dominated by firms in Protestant ownership and encouraged the religious orders and other Church institutions to give their business to Dublin Dairies. It may be coincidence that Dublin Dairies' premises in the Dublin suburb of Kimmage stood close to the McQuaid family motor import business, run by the Archbishop's brother, Matt.'

The Leinster Milk Society took a similar view, confirming that: 'There was no commercial reason why the firm should be launched in a market already showing wasteful competition . . . The objective seems to have been socio-religious rather than business oriented.'

McQuaid's plan worked like a dream and, inside fifteen years, Dublin Dairies had come from nowhere to grab 27 per cent of the milk market in the capital, before merging with Merville and Tel-el-Kebir to make ice cream under the Premier label. A crucial factor in getting Dublin Dairies out of the starting blocks, according to the Leinster Milk Society, was that: 'A large number of [Catholic] religious institutions changed their accounts to the new firm.'

1940S
TOP 5 SWEETS

1 ANISEED BALLS

In the war years of shortages, sweet eaters were forced to go back to basics, and aniseed balls were one of the comforting old reliables. Made by layering sugar around a rapeseed, aniseed oil provides the strong flavour.

2 BARLEY STICKS

An age-old favourite, hard barley sticks were made for licking and could last for ages. As the authorities made plans to evacuate Belfast's schoolchildren from the city to the country, they ordered 60,000 barley sticks for the children's lunchboxes.

3 CHOC ICE

The first choc ice was sold in the United States in 1921, consisting of a rectangle of chocolate-covered vanilla ice cream without a stick. In 1948, HB launched Ireland's first choc ice wrapped in silver and gold foil and also without a stick.

4 ROCK

Rock is made from the cheapest and most basic ingredients, but the process of pulling and kneading the elastic sugary dough is slow and time-consuming. Because the basics, granulated sugar and glucose syrup, remained available during the Emergency, the rock-makers stayed in business.

5 POLO MINTS

These were introduced by Rowntree's in 1948, with Polo Fruits hot on their heels. The distinctive hole in the middle didn't appear until 1955. The name reportedly came from 'polar' to represent coolness.

CHAPTER FOUR

1950S
BACK IN BUSINESS

After a decade of sugar rationing, black-marketeering, slump and uncertainty, the sweetshop owners of Ireland attempted to regain lost ground at the start of the 1950s. A recruitment call went out for confectioners to join together to meet 'the urgent and pressing need for trade protection'.

The aim of the Confectioners' and Fruitiers' Association was to turn back the clock to a time when they could sell their goods at a handsome profit without facing 'unfair competition' from tobacconists, drapers, publicans, door-to-door salesmen, travelling shops and other assorted chancers.

The association listed some of its achievements over the previous twenty-five years. These included:

'One. The complete withdrawal of automatic machines for the sale of sweets and chocolates, which were intended to be placed in public thoroughfares in all districts. The association compelled some of the largest manufacturers to end these schemes. Two. The prevention of the sales of boxes of chocolates by certain shops and stores not in the trade during the Christmas season and other periods of the year. Three. The association has taken active steps to stop price cutting and nothing will be left undone to wipe out this evil.'

But there was no stopping the tide of change, however

slow it was lapping over a country becalmed in economic doldrums.

Sweetshop owners, who still considered themselves the only legitimate confectioners in the country, still poured loose sweets from big glass jars onto weighing scales before scooping them into a bag or wrapping them in a cone of newspaper. Of course, if a weighing machine was 'off' by half an ounce, it might result in the shopkeeper making a large inadvertent profit over the course of the year by selling light measures. Perish the thought.

There was no scope for such happy accidents with the new cellophane-wrapped assortment packages that were soaring in popularity with cinema goers and were popping up in all types of non-sweetshops. One confectioner complained bitterly that prepacked boxes of Liquorice Allsorts were driving the 'professional confectioner' out of the cinema lobbies, where he was no longer required with his weighing machine and assorted jars of loose sweets.

And yet, as the 1950s kicked off, the confectionery trade in Ireland was thriving, with scores of small factories all over the country making sweets for the domestic, and sometimes the purely local, market.

Dublin's city centre was chock-a-block with sweet makers all within a stone's throw of each other. Celtic Confections of Hardwicke Street specialised in its 'famous Dublin Souvenir Rock'. Nearby, Bland & Grant produced Milk Whipped Cream Walnuts, Chocolate Dates, Milk Chocolate Macaroons and numerous other lines. Royal Candy of Montague Court advertised their Fruit Lolly Pop for one penny, a Milk Chocolate Toastie for twopence and their Crisp Crunch Bar, which was a blatant knock-off of Cadbury's Crispy Crunch, for threepence. Meanwhile the Dublin Toffee Company of Summerhill offered a new range of one penny and twoppenny lines 'for the kiddies'. Elsewhere, Jacob's, more famous for their biscuits, were staying active in the sweets market with promotions for their Klondyke and Tucan bars.

In the world of ice cream, HB had a big hit on its hands with the recently launched Choc Ice, which was still a work in progress because, while it came wrapped in foil, it, as yet, didn't have a stick. The equally successful Golly Bar was also in the pipeline. In Cork, the citizens were told in adverts that locally made Polar ice creams were 'worth sprinting for'.

Meanwhile, the president of Galway Chamber of Commerce, D.D. Coyle, was outlining the possibility that the abundance of seaweed all along the western seaboard, known as carrageenan, could be exploited as an ingredient in the global manufacture of ice cream. He said that, as he spoke, Ms Máirín de Valera was in Brittany to inspect their seaweed-processing plants.

But while the trade waited for Ms de Valera's return,

Damian Corless

SWEET MEMORIES
SEAN FOSSIL, THE 1940s AND 1950s

In old money, there were 240 pennies in a pound. Here's a list of sweets we could get in the 1950s for one old penny, or 1d.

    10 toffee Honey Bees.

    2 pieces of Cleeves toffee, very hard unwrapped toffee.

    12 aniseed balls, very small hard sweets with a little seed in the middle.

    1 gobstopper, another ball only big and very hard.

    A Cough No More bar, black toffee.

    Giftee bar, regular toffee.

    Sailor's Chew, toffee bar with nuts.

    More expensive options costing maybe 2d or 3d were:

    A packet of candy cigarettes.

    Nutty chews.

A big treat was to get a packet of Spangles from England when relations came home from there – a rare occurrence as emigrants didn't get home very often. Later on, this hard fruit sweet was sold in Ireland as Gems.

Before there was a local shop in our estate, the only access to sweets we had was the bag of mixed loose sweets Mam used to buy once a week in Woolworth's in the Henry Street Arcade. We were allowed one sweet a day and that was it.

---

the future had already arrived in the shape of a new ice lolly, Whistlepops. One trade plugger enthused: 'Flavours and colours are all very well, it seems, but what really delights the younger generation is noise! So whistle lolly sticks have arrived.'

      ೞ   ೞ   ೞ   ೞ

There was an old guy – at least he seemed old to us kids – named Charlie who had a three-wheeled motorbike with a big box attached at the front full of sweets. He would go from one estate to the next most days, selling his wares. Charlie would blow the horn and the kids would come running to buy a bar or any of the sweets mentioned above – if they had the money. Those of us without a penny or even a halfpenny would look enviously at the delights on offer with drooling tongues.

I remember when I was older – maybe fourteen or fifteen – going into Woolworth's with some guys from school and robbing a bar of Cadbury's chocolate. Oh the thrill of getting away with it – if we had been caught there would have been absolute hell to pay and the fear we would have wound up in Artane Industrial School. But then came the guilt afterwards and the dread of having to confess the sin to the priest. I can't remember if I did or not – but I do know that it was the beginning and end of my career in robbing. And I don't think I've tasted sweeter chocolate since!

1950s Assortment

For Personal Use Only

With a deeply Freudian typo, the *Evening Herald* reported that the census of 1951 was 'the biggest census of copulation ever taken in the State'. Not quite, but the population survey provided proof positive that tens of thousands of mostly young Irish people were emigrating each year to work in British factories, and toil as navvies and labourers rebuilding England's bombed-out roads and cities.

As they watched impotently as the flower of the nation's youth took the cattle boat to England, Ireland's Church and state leaders were indeed highly concerned about any copulation that might be going on in pagan Britain. While the Dáil debated the possibility of preventing young girls from leaving the country, civil servants were busy completing a report on the scope for 'incidents of immorality' amongst the Irish swarming to Britain, and Irish newspapers carried reports of married men leaving their wives and kids at home and starting up a secret second family in England.

But while the politicians and churchmen were getting in a tizzy about mortal sin, most of those travelling to Britain to work or to visit relatives were concerned with more mundane forms of law breaking.

For instance, a much-asked question at the start of the 1950s was: 'How many sweets can I legally take into Britain?'

The wartime rationing of sweets in Britain wouldn't be lifted until February 1953, followed by sugar in September of that year and meat in July 1954.

Such was the clamour for information from would-be law-abiding Irish citizens with family in Britain that, in December 1952 the Minister for Industry and Commerce Seán Lemass issued guidelines for Christmas gifts being posted or carried to Britain.

A bewildering maze of rules and regulations had come into being since Irish independence governing what items could and could not legally pass between the two states, and these continued to baffle long after the end of the Second World War.

The minister said that under Irish law, it was okay to send presents of jams, cakes, sweets and chocolates 'provided they are sent by parcel post'. Lemass added that, with the kind permission of the Minister for Agriculture, it was also permitted to send certain foodstuffs to family and friends in England without having to get an export licence. Gifts which could be mailed included 'one turkey, one goose, one duck or fowl, fresh fruit, fresh vegetables, tinned vegetables, fish (other than salmon) and honey'.

However, the minister took pains to point out that there were other foodstuffs freely available in Ireland which would be seized by British customs if anyone was foolish enough to try to send or carry them in food parcels. The banned list included canned fruits, dried fruits, chocolates and all sugar confectionery. The minister also stressed that it was illegal for family members or friends in Britain to send cash to Ireland in return for chocolates or sweets.

In February 1953, the British government finally relaxed its ban on sweet and chocolate imports from Ireland, but it remained illegal to bring in or mail dried or canned fruits. And Irish travellers to Britain were reminded that they could only bring in confectionery where the customs officers were satisfied that 'the quantities are reasonable, that they are for personal use, and are not being imported for merchandise or for sale'.

Because of the proximity of Ireland and the sheer volume of Irish citizens flooding into Britain, Irish travellers were heavily discriminated against in terms of the number of sweets they could carry. Passengers stepping off a ship from the Republic of Ireland were restricted to carrying seven pounds of food stuffs, with no one item to weigh more than two pounds. Passengers landing from all other destinations could carry fifty pounds of food stuffs with an individual piece weighing up to ten pounds.

Television Parties

In the 1950s, there was still a seasonal element to the making of ice cream, and even chocolate. In May 1953, the *Sunday Press* reported that, thanks to a combination of mild weather and a big spurt in the growth of grass, all of the country's chocolate-factory workers had been put on overtime. According to the newspaper: 'Dublin's chocolate factories are taking on more and more hands in order to keep working right around the clock to cope with the greatest supply of surplus milk that ever flowed into Dublin. One city supplier said: "I've never seen anything like it."'

A couple of weeks later in June, the people of Britain had never seen anything quite like it when they watched television pictures of the coronation of their new queen, Elizabeth II. Tens of thousands of new television sets were bought by first-time owners in Britain and, in Ireland, the small few who had sets tuned in for a free peek at the BBC's coverage.

The well-heeled owners of television sets along the eastern seaboard of Ireland could receive BBC broadcasts from Yorkshire, although depending on the atmospherics, the reception could often resemble gazing at a novelty snowstorm in a fish tank. In 1953, the BBC opened its Northern Ireland service and the signal spilled over the border into the Republic's northern counties.

Meanwhile, the Republic's political masters were debating whether they should open a television service, not because they had anything they wanted to screen, but so that the Republic would not be seen to be lagging behind the North in technological advancement.

In the Dáil, the minister in charge of communications, Erskine Childers, said that the coming of television was 'inevitable, like the motor car'. However, he warned that Ireland shouldn't rush into a 'hasty' embrace of 'this greatest propaganda force for good or evil in the modern world'. When the minister warned that television could bring 'vulgarity' into Irish households, a deputy from the southeast said that people in Wicklow Town had been watching the BBC for some years with 'a good reception' and he felt that the Irish people could be trusted that if they ever were confronted with shows 'of a vulgar type . . . they would not tolerate them for five minutes'.

As usual, as all this high-minded waffle was going on, the plain people of Ireland were crowding into each other's living rooms for a glimpse at the new miracle box, providing sweet sellers with an opening. With the coronation of 1953 giving television a boost in Ireland as well as neighbouring Britain, the Irish confectioners' trade magazine noted 'a striking demand for sweets' to coincide with the new craze for 'television parties'.

It advised its members: 'One of the consequences of this new amenity is the growing prevalence of what may be described as television parties, the gathering together, that is to say, of a number of neighbours to view a television programme.'

Since it was considered bad manners to turn up at someone's door without some small gift, friends and neighbours were arriving with bags of sweets to share.

'This is a tendency which the confectionery industry should do all it can, by way of advertising and display in the shop, to encourage. Impulse sales of sweets – and continued growth of turnover will largely depend on impulse – must inevitably be enhanced by propaganda of this kind.'

Whatever Happened to Lucky Balls?

Writing for his fellow confectioners, one H. Lomley pondered that while liquorice was still widely available in string form, known as bootlaces, 'the liquorice pipe seems to be falling into disrepute'. Lamenting that 'nowadays one must hunt far afield for a liquorice pipe', Lomley turned his attention to another favourite which seemed to have disappeared from the jars behind the sweetshop counter.

He asked: 'What has happened to those crimson, sugar-coated Lucky Balls which were the delight of our youth? Here was real value for money as not alone did a child obtain something to keep it chewing for a lengthy period, but there was also a chance of receiving a 'money back guarantee' as well! Someone with a killjoy attitude to life has told me that for reasons of safety, the practice of putting coins in suchlike confections was dispensed with. There was always the danger, said my informant, that a child would swallow the penny or halfpenny contained in the Lucky Balls. This, of course, is the sheerest rubbish. Show me the child that will swallow a coin whilst fully aware that the sweet it is sucking may actually contain just that object.'

And he wasn't finished his trip down memory lane.

He rued 'another departed custom which gave endless pleasure – and indeed educative information too – to our children'. This departed custom was the one of giving away collectable cards in packs of cigarettes. He wrote: 'What pride of possession one experienced when, at the eleventh hour, a long-sought-after numbered card was discovered to complete a series of Dogs or Horses, Wild Flowers or Old Cries of London. If any manufacturers ever decide to reissue cards, either old or new sets, then I fear I shall immediately become a chain smoker.'

Happily, in the very next issue of the journal, Mr Lomley was delighted to report that the Dublin Toffee Company had risen to his 'challenge' and was hard at work putting deadly objects into children's sweets. He gushed: '[The] whole place seems to be concentrating on turning out these crimson sugar-coated sweetmeats. Small coins, paper wrapped, are being inserted into a good percentage of them.'

With food rationing a very recent memory, and millions across post-war Europe going to bed hungry every night, confectionery bars continued to be heavily marketed for their nutritional value as much as their luxury status. Cadbury's long-running 'Bridge That Gap' ad campaign pitched their Dairy Milk bars as the meal you can eat between meals.

But there was, apparently, even better to come. While H. Lomley was taking a misty-eyed look back at the sweets of old, another writer in his magazine was confidently predicting that within ten short years the appliance of science would develop 'a candy bar that will produce a balanced diet all by itself'.

He wrote: 'It would have its advantages. You wouldn't have to rush the good woman to prepare an early dinner on the days you would be going to a football match. All you will have to do would be to put one of these 'super' candy bars in your pocket and eat your dinner at half-time. Or if you met some of your friends after church, you wouldn't have to worry about the wife's efforts to keep your dinner warm. However, the Americans may do what they like but we imagine somehow that Irishmen will still vote for roast beef or a nice piece of juicy corned beef.'

Sweets, Health and Slimming: Goodbye to the Lemon Cult

The shopping bible for the well-to-do Irish housewife at the start of the twentieth century was *Lady of the House* magazine, which featured articles and adverts running the gamut from grand pianos to gourmet dog food. In it, the most upmarket stores advertised their finest ranges of sweets, chocolates, cocoa drinks and biscuits. The advertisers offered to post free samples of confectionery to any reader who sent them a stamped addressed envelope, provided they could furnish a 'good' address.

Peppered amongst the adverts for sweets were others aimed at those battling their sweet tooth. One boasted 'All Fat People Can Be Cured By Taking Trilene Tablets'. Another appealed to readers who were 'Too Stout', to try Dr Grey's Fat Reducing Pills which were 'a special preparation for hunting men, jockeys and stubborn cases [either sex] which have resisted other treatment'.

Even as these preparations were being marketed as miracle slimming aids, the *British Medical Journal* was dismissing them as 'useless'. Dr Grey's medication was mostly sulphur, while Trilene tablets contained small amounts of seaweed and starch, but were 87 per cent made up of the slimmer's deadliest enemy – sugar.

While Dr Grey's Fat Reducing Pills were marketed at hunting men and jockeys, women were the main target of the slimming industry from the outset. When the boyish flapper look became the style that defined the Roaring Twenties, a dismayed sugar industry blamed women for causing a global sugar glut.

According to a 1926 Irish newspaper report headlined 'Women's Craze To Be Thin': 'At present there is a world glut of sugar, and the fact that vast stores of it are lying idle and unwanted by consumers may find a possible explanation in the fact that women who wish to reduce their weight are refusing sugar in any shape or form. As it is fashionable to be thin, it may be estimated that at least a quarter of the female population is adhering to the non-sugar diet.'

The report quoted a sugar executive who remarked:

'We noticed a difference in this trade soon after this 'get-thin-quick' craze began, but we find consolation in the belief that it cannot last very long. No woman – not even a stout one – can resist the lure of chocolate indefinitely.'

Just two years later, with the flapper on the point of extinction, the sugar trade rejoiced that the slimming craze was over for good.

Likening the women slimmers to the returning prodigal son of the Bible, one report declared: 'Fashionable women are at last saying goodbye to the lemon cult and other slimming processes, and chocolate and sweet makers are rejoicing. "During the craze for slimness our profits were very bad indeed," said a well-known chocolate maker. "When one thinks of bulk and how to reduce it the very first banned eatable is chocolate. Now curves are coming back the trade is materially improved. Customers we knew before starving was fashionable have returned."'

Ten years down the line, starving was again in fashion. Readers of *The Irish Times'* woman's page were instructed: 'One of the best ways to slim, according to an eminent obesity specialist, is to remain in bed, under a doctor's supervision, for two to three weeks absolutely without food, drinking only water and orange juice. But even though most women desire to be slim, very few are in a position to afford the luxury of such a treatment. For, though it may not cost anything in food over that period, it does necessitate a domestic upheaval such as few can contemplate.'

With food stuffs rationed and sweets in short supply in the 1940s, there was little talk of slimming, but by the mid-1950s weight loss was back on the agenda and the US candy giants were in a tizzy as consumption there plummeted.

Damian Corless

SWEET MEMORIES
June Considine, The 1950s

By the age of five in the 1950s, I had decided to marry my cousin. Gerry lived around the corner from me, was my elder by two weeks and he was equally enthusiastic about our forthcoming nuptials. However, before we headed for the altar, we had to get certain practicalities out of the way, our education being the main stumbling block.

On our first day in school, we found an empty desk, sat down together and ignored the pandemonium surrounding us. But two boys who lived near us also decided to share our space. I clung grimly to the edge of the desk as the boys inspected each other's lunch bags and became quite emotional over cheese triangles and soggy tomato sandwiches.

When Sr Mary Bride had restored order and calmed the weeping first-timers, she descended on our desk and informed me that I had to sit with the girls. I was horrified and squeezed closer to my future husband. When the teacher insisted that my rightful place was on the girls' side of the classroom, I resorted to a tactic I learned at the moment of birth – loud and prolonged wails.

Sister Bride, who wore a black veil, rattling rosary beads and a long leather strap, believed in bribery. As my tears splashed on the desk, she rummaged in the folds of her habit and produced a Nutty Favourite. It was shaped like a mushroom and worked like magic. My tears stopped instantly as I weighed up the price of true love against this coconut-coated inducement. Needless to say, the Nutty Favourite won out.

Throughout my childhood, I chewed my way through enough slabs of Cleeves toffee to pave the M50. I sucked enough cough drops to supply the HSE with an anti-flu vaccine and the ridges on my teeth are, according to my dentist, the result of my addiction to acid drops.

I smoked candy cigarettes from the age of four and cared for a jelly baby in a matchbox (this was the pre-Tamagotchi era), and *was deeply traumatised when a cousin (not the above mentioned) found the box and ate my baby.*

Woolworth's was the Mecca of the sweet kingdom. The variety of pick and mix sweets on display drew me like a magnet. In Ireland of the fifties, where sweets were usually displayed on high shelves in large glass jars, having them within hand's reach was a wonderful novelty — and one that caused many wayward hands to reach out to grab a bar of chocolate or a fistful of bull's eyes.

But the local sweetshop was where pocket money was usually spent and significant transactions, ranging from a penny to sixpence, were carried out. The clang of the cash register was constant and I still remember the ornate weighing scales with their wide angular heads and tiny weights. A paper spill of Honey Bees could be bought for a penny, a Flash Bar, if I remember correctly, was twopence and, once the chocolate was licked off, it could be chewed indefinitely.

The faraway hills were always greener and the fact that Spangles were only available in England gave them an added flavour. My father, who was a ship's cook, always bought them for us when the ship docked in Liverpool. My English cousins who spoke with exotic Midlands' accents, and smoked in my bedroom behind their mother's back, also flashed the Spangles and filled me with a longing to emigrate.

Today, I bring my grandchildren to The Really Old Sweetshop in Malahide where plastic jars replicate the old-fashioned glass ones. The sweet selection is vast. There are some old reminders but mainly they have unfamiliar names, and strange shapes, textures and sizes. The only thing that has not changed, and never will, is the shiny-eyed excitement and the furrowed brow of a new generation as they make their choices and establish their memories for the future.

As usual, women were blamed.

An Irish confectionery journal reported: 'In America, the confectionery trade, together with other industries using sugar, have recently been hit by a remarkable slimming craze over there. It's not like the Americans, however, to sit down calmly and allow their industrial activity to be hindered for long, even by women. They have struck back with the inevitable education campaign. Nearly $2 million have been subscribed by those industries supplying sugar to the community in order to teach the US women the place of sugar in a balanced diet.'

Full-page adverts were taken out by Sugar Information Inc. urging people to have a regular 'scientific nibble' of sweets to control their appetite. Using an image of the dainty hummingbird, Sugar Information Inc. ran a parallel campaign targeting weight-watchers with the message: 'Sugar helps prevent you from overeating. With sugar in your diet, you're happier with smaller portions of everything.'

It was as part of this $2 million propaganda campaign that the marketing genius Dr Ernest Dichter came up with the suggestion to divide candy bars into smaller squares, persuading customers that these bite-sized portions could be eaten guilt free. The Mars company conducted its own research and came up with an alternative strategy, where the customer was told it was okay to reward themselves for any job well done.

Mars gave its M&M line of button-sized sweets a new marketing push with the slogan: 'To make that tough job easier, you deserve M&M Candy.'

It worked a treat. Sales of M&Ms doubled in test areas.

It's all in the mind.

Chewing Gum: Shop Girls and Typists, Spitting and Chewing

Chewing gum as we know it today arrived in Ireland from America at the end of the nineteenth century. Made from a latex substance called chicle from the sapodilla tree, New York No.1 was a flavourless gum first mass-marketed by a photographer and jack of all trades called Thomas Adams in 1871. In 1884, Adams added liquorice to the mix and his Adams' Black Jack caused a taste sensation. Within a few years, Adams was fighting off stiff competition from Dentyne, Chiclets and a brace of blockbusters unleashed by Thomas Wrigley Junior in the form of his Wrigley's Spearmint and Juicy Fruit lines.

In 1929, the government TD Dr Thomas Hennessy turned to his own party colleague, Public Health Minister General Richard Mulcahy, and asked him to ban the sale of chewing gum in the Irish Free State because of the 'demoralisation and injury to health' it was causing to young people.

The minister said no.

Six months later, in 1930, Dr Hennessy was banging on once again in the Dáil about the dangers to the youth of chewing gum. In an era when unpasteurised milk was spreading tuberculosis and rogue ice cream makers were poisoning people, the medic charged that chewing gum was a major carrier of disease. He told the Dáil:

'Lately, I noticed that some children leaving school invested in chewing gum. The great drawback of chewing gum is that the gum is indestructible. This piece of chewing gum passed around from mouth to mouth amongst a dozen school children. Each of them had their suck out of it. It struck me that if there was one child with infectious disease in the group how easily the disease would be spread amongst all the others. Infectious disease has been spread amongst school children in that way.'

Even as Hennessy was spelling out this threat to colleagues who didn't seem to care much, a company called British Chewing Sweets was preparing to launch a major promotional drive in Ireland for its Oh Boy Gum. Advising its members that an Oh Boy sales rep would soon come calling, the confectioners' trade journal said: 'We may expect to see shortly the Oh Boys boys all dressed up around the schools and factories in our town.'

The invention of modern chewing gum coincided almost precisely with the birth of the typewriter and its rapid spread went hand in hand with a deluge of young women into the workplace to man those early twentieth-century sweatshops known as typing pools. No sooner had young women gained this new visibility behind a desk than they were being sullied in print, on comic postcards and on the silver screen as flappers, slappers and potential home wreckers.

Chewing gum was seized upon as a glaring sign of low standards in a woman. In 1913, *The Irish Times* stated that 'shop girls and typists' were responsible for an increase in 'the practice of spitting on the pavement and gum chewing'.

In 1923, the same paper had reported a convention speaker as saying: 'The chewing of gum makes the modern girl's face as hard as the crockery of a railroad lunch counter. Human beings were not meant to be ruminating animals, and, when they try it, there is some kind of a rebellion of nature and the muscles of the jaw become unduly enlarged.'

Chewing gum had been one of the traits of the 'flapper', that threatening breed of 1920s woman who smoked, drank, wore short skirts, bobbed their hair

and bopped to jazz. The puritans running the newly independent Irish Free State despised and detested these scandalous free spirits – mainly in principle, since sightings were rare in Ireland – and they would have been overjoyed to read a 1928 *Irish Times* story headlined 'Reported Death Of The Flapper'.

It began: 'Gone is the flapper. In her place has come the young woman with poise of soft-toned and correct speech, soberly dressed and without closely cropped hair.' As the last rites were being said for 'these hard-boiled little things with shaved necks', readers were reminded: 'Her hair overnight resembled that of a Hottentot, her skirts ended about her knees, she sneaked her brother's cigarettes and swore like a trooper. She chewed gum – great wads of it – vigorously and incessantly. Her make-up was as crude as a clown's.'

Although the flapper did indeed disappear down an evolutionary cul-de-sac, the sight of young women chewing gum was here to stay as Irish cinema audiences aped the habits of their silver-screen idols.

However, the scare story that gum chewing could lead to a 'Desperate Dan jaw' did take root, and 'An Irishman's Diary' reported in 1931 that women were practising in front of a mirror 'to gain the correct "chewing gum smile" and care must be taken to use different sides of the mouth in order that the muscles on one side may not become enlarged'.

But if an addiction to chewing gum was seen by polite society as a sign of indecency in a girl, it was more often used to signify criminality in a male. The newspapers of the 1930s are full of stories of youths charged with stealing jars of gum, and of defendants in court who flaunted their obvious guilt by chewing gum. One report headlined 'Holiday Vandalism' stated that the type of person who'd rip up newly planted trees or set hillsides ablaze was 'akin to those half-developed adults who love to paint misspelled inscriptions on every blank wall and to stick chewing gum on the seats of third-class carriages in order that some unknown victim may sit on it'.

The author was operating on the assumption that the type of people who chewed gum would never have been admitted to first or second class.

Sometimes, chewing gum was even used by criminals as a tool of their trade, as in the case of three Dundalk boys aged eleven to thirteen charged with stealing ninepence from a donation box in a Marist church. The three made the mistake of going back to the well once too often, and on the final occasion a Guard Brennan was hiding in a confession box ready to pounce. To make doubly sure of an arrest, the policeman had placed marked coins in the collection box.

After giving a false name and address in English, and then in Irish, one of the boys admitted that on several occasions he had attached a large piece of well-chewed gum to the end of a school ruler and used it to fish out money through the slot.

According to the court report: 'District Justice Goff said it seemed impossible to believe that Catholic boys did not understand the seriousness of a crime of the kind.' Like many a later judge of the PlayStation era, the judge continued: 'These lads had devices at their fingers' ends which boys in a past age would never have dreamt of. Whether they got these things from the films he did not know, but there was an extraordinary development of sacrilegious criminality.'

When a lawyer for one of the boys informed the judge that the wicked cinema was indeed responsible, the judge lamented: 'It is a scandal. There will be nothing but cinemas in Dublin very soon.'

If the nation's love affair with Hollywood movies

whetted appetites for chewing gum, the disruptions of the Second World War caused a famine of the stuff in Ireland. Gum began to trickle over the border from the North with the huge build-up of US troops there getting ready for the D-Day invasions of 1944, but with the war just ended and the troops going home, the famine returned.

In August 1945, one journalist, in the early stages of giving up smoking, went in search of gum on the streets of Dublin. He wrote: 'There is an elaborate formula for getting chewing gum. First you go to a sweetshop and they say they have had no gum since before the war. They say they wish they had, because it's caught on great. After that, you find an American soldier.'

The writer recorded with delight that he stopped an on-leave Air Force lieutenant on Dawson Street who directed him to another officer staying in the Hibernian Hotel, who supplied him with packs of Juicy Fruit, Beechnut and a wondrous assortment called Five Flavours which did what it said on the label.

The imagery of brave gum-chewing soldiers liberating Europe, combined with a new drive to market gum as a nerve-soothing alternative to smoking, resulted in the product enjoying a far less hostile press after the war than before. Indeed, one story in praise of gum in *The Irish Times* noted approvingly: 'Before Pearl Harbour the average American chewed just over one hundred sticks of gum a year. After it the figure rose to 130.'

The same *Irish Times* story from 1947, headlined 'New Chewing Gum Is Good For Tonsils As Well As Nerves', broke the good news that: 'Penicillin chewing gum is the latest delectable to be put on the market. The penicillin in a measured dose is combined with the gum and the resultant combination is not just good for the gums of the chewer, but especially for the tonsils of children.'

And then the bad news: 'The gum has to be masticated for seven hours.'

Official Ireland finally embraced chewing gum in 1953 when a factory was fitted out in the Dublin satellite town of Dún Laoghaire, employing a grateful workforce of some one hundred at a time when every cattle boat to England was packed with those fleeing the zombie economy.

In 1955, the firm John O. Barker Ltd launched Bubbledoon, a novelty bubblegum aimed at capturing the Irish-American market, even though its makers admitted that trying to sell bubblegum to the Yanks was 'like bringing coals to Newcastle'. Selling for one penny a stick in Ireland, and the cent equivalent in the States, the gum was moulded to look like a large coin, stamped on one side with a harp and on the other with the legend 'Bubbledoon – Made in Ireland'.

Bubbledoon was not to last, but in 1959 another bubblegum venture opened in the County Kildare town of Kilcock which is still in business today. On a tour of North America in 1957, Dublin's Lord Mayor and Fianna Fáil TD Robert Briscoe managed to convince the Leaf family of Chicago to set up a bubblegum factory in Ireland. The factory opened with Briscoe as one of its directors. The plant closed in 1978 with the loss of 220 jobs, but a re-launched venture was taken over by Zed Candy in 1999, an Irish firm that keeps today's youngsters chewing hard with its range of jawbreakers, golf balls, eye poppers, bubble kings and fizz bombs.

Get Rid of those Rats

After the decade of economic doldrums that spanned the entire 1940s, Ireland's retailers entered the 1950s blinking into what they hoped would be a brighter future, but nothing was going to improve unless they first cleaned up their act.

The country's sweetshops, grocers, butchers, cafés and pubs were, by and large, filthy. When the Dáil debated new laws to enforce better hygiene in 1950, Fianna Fáil's Dr Martin Brennan acknowledged that the Fine Gael-led coalition had 'embarked on a campaign [for] the eradication of one of our greatest enemies, the simple little fly'.

But, insisted Brennan, the government's campaign to clean up filthy shops had been half-hearted. He said: 'I suggest that the minister [Dr Noël Browne] should take much more stringent measures than have already been taken in trying to eradicate that pest. He has only to go to any of our restaurants or cafés and he will see there an abundance of these insects circling everywhere, on the food and the milk, contaminating the food and probably spreading disease.'

Shortly afterwards, Dr James Ryan replaced Browne as Minister for Health and he warned that new food hygiene regulations would be strictly enforced from 1 April 1952. He added that Ireland's army of small-time ice cream makers would be brought under control, and that all must now register and open up for inspections. Ryan then addressed those responsible for cleaning up Ireland's shops. He told the members of the Health Inspectors' Association that every one of them had 'come across food premises infested with rats and mice' and run by 'unclean' shopkeepers. They must now deal once and for all with these filthy shopkeepers, although he stressed that this must be done through 'firmness tempered with friendliness'.

The minister and his health inspectors knew they had a battle on their hands. According to the trade journal, one inspector had asked more than one hundred shopkeepers

to cease displaying unwrapped and uncovered sweets and cakes in windows and on open counters.

However: 'Opposition from several shopkeepers was considerable. They felt it was an interference with privileges they had enjoyed for many years. If sweets had to be protected from contamination, they should arrive at their shops with protection already provided by the manufacturers.'

Of course, this was nonsense, since sweetshop owners spent much of their time protesting about the spread of wrapped and packaged sweets which deprived them of the opportunity to weigh out light measures.

The Confectioners' Association generally supported its paid-up members to the hilt, no matter how daft or unreasonable their stance, but this time the association recognised that the government was in the right.

An editorial in *The Irish Tobacco and Sweets Review* appeared under the headline 'A Word For The Retailer'. Its writer reflected: 'I've seen a score of windows lately with dead flies and moths dying about all over the place. You might think they make your sweets look more appetising but, take it from me, they don't. Would you buy cakes from a place which had dead insects lying around the pastries? You know you wouldn't, so why should people buy sweets from your fly mortuary?

'Take your window out. From the look of it, it's been in far too long anyway. Give the inside of the window glass a good polish, throw out all those fly-speckled showcards and put in a fresh show, clean and bright.

'Too much trouble? They'll still come in no matter what your window looks like? Don't believe it! You want to get out of that frame of mind before it's too late, friend. Those days are over. Now we're off the ration, trade is better, I know, but on the other hand customers are getting more finicky.

'Someone once said that dirty people patronise dirty shops. If you want that sort of trade, you're welcome. And I hope the sanitary inspector catches up with you. And you don't have to tell me that dirty people's money is as good as anyone else's. I know it is. But dirty people patronising a dirty shop limit its trade to dirty people. There are far more clean people about than dirty ones, and clean people will not go into a dirty shop.

'The trouble is that far too many of us are far too used to the sight of our shops. It's time we looked at them as strangers would. That piece of glass missing from your counter showcase no longer seems to you the eyesore it really is. That crepe paper over there has been faded for ages but you haven't noticed it. Pull it down.'

A subsequent edition of the same publication took an even bolder approach to tackling filth in the country's sweetshops. Headlined 'Get Rid Of Those Rats', it opened by explaining: 'Now, Mister Rat is a very cunning enemy and if he is to be evicted a great deal of strategy must be employed.'

The writer went on to point out that rats are not idiots, and needed to be lulled into a false sense of

1950S
TOP 5 SWEETS

1 TAYTO CRISPS

In 1954, entrepreneur Joe Murphy founded the Tayto company in Dublin and set his star employee Seamus Burke the task of inventing the world's first flavoured potato crisp. Working on a kitchen table, Burke came up with cheese and onion, and the world's top crisp executives flocked to Dublin to learn the trick and buy the rights.

2 GOLLY BAR

The first Golly bars rolled off the production line at HB in Dublin in 1957. Ice creams on a stick were still a novelty in Ireland, so the wrapper of the first Golly bars proudly boasted in large print that they were 'on a stick'.

3 LUCKY BALLS

Large, hard balls like toffee gobstoppers, these red globules produced by the Dublin Toffee Company offered kids the chance of chewing their way down to a coin hidden in the middle. Those who objected that these concealed coins could be lethal were dismissed by those in the trade as 'killjoys'.

4 SPANGLES

In the 1950s, it was part of the weekend ritual for countless Irish kids to go to the local cinema on Saturday mornings for Boy's Own action movies like *Flash Gordon*, *The Lone Ranger* and *Hopalong Cassidy*. Mars launched Spangles in 1950 as 'Hoppy's favourite sweet'.

5 MACAROON BARS

First manufactured in 1937 by Wilton Candy in County Kildare, the Macaroon bar was a casualty of the war in the 1940s when the essential ingredient of coconut could no longer be readily found in Ireland. Normal service was resumed in the 1950s.

SWEET MEMORIES
SEAN O'CONNOR, THE 1950s

Boyhood life in the 1950s Francis Street in the Liberties of Dublin was sweet. Mrs Meenan's shop facing Nicholas of Myra Church was the epicentre of my young years. She sold sweets and second-hand comics and kept slot machines.

These three temptations were interwoven in a way all businesses should copy. When you sold a second-hand comic you could buy sweets or — better for Mrs Meenan — lose your payment on the slots. If you entered the premises with money already on your person, you could buy sweets, or a comic, or both, or try the slots.

Nobody had much money.

What you got from your relations on your Communion day could be spent in a spree on lucky bags or conversation lozenges (these would exhort you to 'Love One Another' or 'Kiss Me Quick'). But the true merits of this local school of economics arose when you had a little pocket money.

For instance, Uncle Joe and Uncle Paddy both gave me a penny every Saturday. But it cost four pence to get in to the Tivoli for the pictures. The twopence you had been given thus became the object of intense financial speculation. You could get Cleeves toffee at a halfpenny each in Meenan's. Four slabs of Cleeves equalled four days of blissful slobbering

security before they would eat any rat poison laid down for them. This must be done by putting out 'pre-baiting mixtures' on the shop floor at night. These might include wholemeal soaked in water, 'stale bread mixed with water to the consistency of porridge', and 'eight parts of flour to one of sugar thoroughly mixed'.

After four nights of happily nibbling the harmless stuff, the rats should suspect nothing when the next batch laid down carries a lethal payload.

while trying to pull your jaws apart. On the other hand, if you tried the slots on a two-to-one chance, you might win and increase your store to threepence. With threepence now in your possession, Ma would lend  *you another penny so you could make it to the pictures, but a penny was her limit. If you lost, then you still had a penny, and that would buy sweets.*

Decisions, always decisions!

I took the way of danger and excitement. I went straight for the slots. When I lost, I consoled myself with a bag of sticky sweets, purchased with the remaining lonely penny. But when I won, I could have sweets, comic and the funds to go again, or maybe borrow that penny for the pictures. That's the story of my life. If you have anything going for you, go for it! But have a fall-back position.

That should always have an in-built consolation of sweets. Sugary, sticky and designed to keep you happy. At least for a little while.

Reflecting on all the sweet sellers she'd encountered over the 1956 August Bank Holiday weekend which had just gone by, the question of hygiene entered the head of newspaper columnist Eve Ireland. She wrote: 'It's strange to reflect that you can go into a sweetshop and buy almost any variety of sweet, chocolate or candy, yet you never get to know a candy maker, sweet boiler or a chocolate dipper. One has a personal contact with the butcher, and in some cases with the baker, and the fishmonger. But the candy maker? Where does he live, move and have his being?'

The columnist concluded that the reason for the secrecy in 1956 was the same as it had been years earlier when the American Jacob Friedman had visited Ireland while researching his classic book *The Common Sense Candy Teacher*.

When he put pen to paper, Friedman had the same judgement to make on the sweet makers of Ireland, Britain and America.

'Why did he [the proprietor] order the door shut? Was there too much draft? No. Was the dust being blown in? No. Was it for fear flies would get in? No. He ordered the door closed because he didn't want his customers to get a sight of the shop. Why didn't he want the customers to see the shop? He wanted the door kept closed for fear his customers would see the filthy condition of his shop. Because he didn't want his customers to see his candy maker and his helpers walking around the shop half-naked, and with what little they did have on would stand alone if taken off.'

Off Their Trollies

Under policies of self-sufficiency and protectionism the economy had ground to a standstill by 1957, and when the entrepreneurial spirit did make a rare appearance at Dublin's Mater Hospital that year, there was an unholy rush to extinguish it.

Trader James O'Flanagan received permission to wheel a trolley around the wards, selling sweets, biscuits and other goods to patients and visitors. The local sweetshop owners had a hissy fit and demanded he be put out of business because he was 'an unwarranted encroachment' on their patch.

Members of RGDATA, the grocers' lobby group,

mounted a picket of the hospital and the trolley was briefly stopped in its tracks. However, two days later O'Flanagan was back doing his rounds and in the process of collecting the signatures of 300 patients and visitors on a petition to allow him to continue in his bedside manner.

The local sweetshop owners sulked that they had no objection to shops opening on the hospital grounds, so long as they were 'run by patients for patients', and so long as they didn't operate during visiting hours.

Common sense was the victor.

Holiday Camps and Seaside Rock

As the 1930s dawned, holidaying habits in Ireland began to change. The principle switch was that, for the first-time, annual holidays became an entitlement for a significant part of the workforce. The introduction of paid holidays for some types of workers dovetailed with a growth in the number of private cars and the opening of new public transport routes. The result was a boost in summer trade for the country's seaside resorts, although one confectioner felt that many service providers seemed to take their standards from Tombstone Gulch.

He wrote: 'The Dublin motor buses now carry crowds of people to many pleasant spots around the city, hitherto inaccessible except to the cyclist or private motorist. The refreshment places available at these places resemble the efforts of early settlers in the Wild West. Surely, there is room for an enterprising city caterer where local initiative is completely lacking.'

Traditionally, the resorts along the eastern seaboard had relied heavily on an influx of trippers from the northwest of England, many of them first-, second- or third-generation Irish coming home to visit kith and kin.

But, according to one report, even these hardy annuals were getting more picky.

'The tourist season has arrived, and thousands of visitors have passed through Dún Laoghaire on their way to different parts of Ireland. Dún Laoghaire traders have a grievance however – that visitors pass through and nothing more! Yet it is stated that recently 1,200 trippers arrived from England and had to go on to Dublin for a meal, because Dún Laoghaire was unprepared.'

Just down the coast from Dún Laoghaire, the good burghers of Bray were also concerned that their old reliables weren't as reliable as they used to be. One fretted: 'Something is wrong in Bray. The number of people who came into Dún Laoghaire this year exceeded by 9,000 the number for the previous year. They represented an expenditure of £30 per head. Bray has not increased its visitors.'

Holidaymakers had been flocking to the Wicklow town of Bray since the 1760s. Many who came for the first century were invalids drawn by the therapeutic benefits of swimming in the sea, and by the nutritional benefits of drinking goats' milk whey which was full of minerals, vitamins and proteins. The railway link to Dublin from the 1850s brought much greater numbers with an insatiable appetite for new sweets like candyfloss and sticks of rock rather than for the health foods of the day.

Sticks of rock with novelty slogans or the name of the resort running through the middle were big seaside sellers throughout Britain and Ireland by the 1930s. Some claim that the first rock with writing inside was being sold on the Isle of Man in 1847 by a man with the very Irish name of Bill Quigeen. The first reliable mention comes from the English writer Henry Mayhew in 1851, who reported that a street seller was doing a roaring trade with sticks of rock which 'when snapped asunder at any part' bore the messages 'Do You Love Me?', 'Lord Mayor's Day' or 'Sir Robert Peel'.

While the rate-paying sweetshop owners of Bray and other Irish resorts did brisk business with sticks of rock, they moaned endlessly about itinerant hawkers walking the strands, the streets and the piers stealing their rightful trade. Nor were the shopkeepers too happy with the growing popularity of candyfloss, which brought yet more competition from fly-by-nights. The first candyfloss machine had been invented in the United States in 1897 and the new Fairy Floss had caused a sensation at the 1904 Louisiana World Fair. By the 1930s, candyfloss was firmly established as an Irish seaside treat.

At a local tourist body meeting to stem the flow of British visitors away from Bray, it was decided to mount a 'drive' through Lancashire and Yorkshire the following spring, circulating every major town with leaflets and guides.

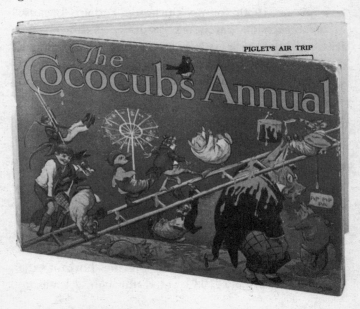

೫ ೫ ೫ ೫

Shortly after the foundation of the Irish Free State in 1922, the new ruling caste made a working grasp of the Irish language compulsory for anyone who sought to climb the ladder of the public service. According to the academic Myles Dillon, this had less to do with a heartfelt love of the native tongue, which was by then hanging on grimly on life support, than with securing a Catholic state for a Catholic people. He insisted that compulsory Irish was used 'as a means of transferring power – or rather authority. At that time all the cultural institutions of the country, except the National University, were in the hands of the Protestants . . . all that must be changed. A new administrative class was to be established and the language was one of the means used.'

The country's leading chocolate maker, Cadbury, was an English firm that had opened a stand-alone Irish base in the 1930s for tax purposes. Perhaps because of its Sassenach parentage, Cadbury embraced the Irish-speaking spirit with gusto and each spring ran a competition for the young members of its Cococubs Club, offering twenty-five lucky winners the chance to holiday for a month in one of the new state-subsidised Gaeltachts springing up around the country.

The country was divided into five regions, with five winners drawn from each. Cadbury ran adverts explaining: 'Members of the club are invited to write an essay in Irish of a story of national interest which is published in the Cococubs paper The Cococub News. A member of Fry-Cadbury staff would correct the essays and writers of the best would be examined orally by Coiste na bPáistí (the Committee of Children).'

With war clouds gathering on the horizon, the government in July 1939 voted through £1,500 to

start up 'a Gaelic holiday camp' at Gibbstown, County Meath, which would 'provide young people in Dublin and district with the opportunity of spending a period in the Gaeltacht without travelling long distances'. The children accepted must be aged twelve and over and speak some Irish already. Boys and girls would be accommodated, but not at the same time. Parents who could scrape together £2 for a child for a fortnight's stay were told: 'The day will be spent at games, excursions, picnics, visits to the Gaeltacht houses, etc. and, at night, ceilidhes, concerts, story-telling etc will be held.'

The local Fine Gael TD, Captain Patrick Giles, was passionately in favour of bringing up the young people to speak Irish. In fact, he believed that the whole future of the country rested on raising children to speak no language other than Irish. He summed up his strongly held views with the statement: 'We have too many cissies in this country.' A 'cissy', for Giles, was a soft city-slicker corrupted by 'the cinemas and books that come in from abroad'. His simple argument was that if future generations of Irish people didn't understand a word of English, they couldn't be turned into cissies by decadent English movies and books.

It's safe to assume that Captain Giles must have choked on his porridge in late 1946 when he opened his morning newspaper to read the headline 'British Holiday Camps To Be Built In Ireland'. The report revealed that Billy Butlin, commander of an army of redcoats, was well advanced with plans to open camping facilities for some 2,000 holiday-makers from Britain, to be waited on hand and foot by Irish workers who would be further infected with what Giles called 'the slave mind'.

Butlin told the press: 'I hope to charter a boat which will sail from either Fishguard or Liverpool each week taking all my holiday-makers together. This camp will be entirely different from my other ventures. It is not my aim to transplant a bit of Wigan to Southern Ireland. I am going to provide a real Irish holiday for those who want it. All the staffs and the bands will be Irish. Food will be a speciality. The holiday-makers will be fed as it is impossible to feed them in England.'

And food was the key for British visitors still facing strict rationing – plentiful steak and pork and chicken and butter and as many sweets, chocolates, cakes and ice creams as the war-weary British visitors could gorge on.

A few months earlier, a reporter from the London *Evening Standard* had joined the big influx of British tourists arriving for the first full summer season following the end of the Second World War. He recorded that some had come for the horse racing, others for the golf and fishing, while some were on the lookout for cheap Irish properties. All, however, had come for the food.

He wrote: 'Every visitor to Dublin lunches at Jammet's Restaurant, which has the best food in town. We ate smoked salmon, a minute steak, asparagus dripping in rich sauce and a peche melba. Not a lot in quantity, but rich in quality. Whereupon we discovered – like every other visitor from England – that we would not be hungry again during our visit. I have never understood calories, but apparently after six years of life in austerity Britain, the digestion just cannot take real food and ask for more. This is the common experience of most British visitors.'

Billy Butlin's plans quickly came to fruition and Butlins Mosney opened on the County Meath coast at the same time as a rival Irish-owned camp began taking guests a few miles down the coast at Red Island, beside the north Dublin seaside town of Skerries.

Captain Giles was deeply disgusted and vented his anger in the *Catholic Standard* in an outburst headlined 'Holiday Camp And Morals'. He asserted: 'Holiday camps are an English idea and are alien and undesirable in an Irish Catholic country – outside influences are bad and dangerous.'

Unable to prevent Butlins Mosney from opening, Giles and some allies in the Catholic hierarchy secured the concession that a church would be built right outside its main gate, with a chaplain as the moral policeman in residence.

The new holiday camps provided regimented entertainment for the social class described by an *Irish Times* wag as 'the frayed-collar worker'. Their social betters believed that the camps were potential vice dens built on a grand scale. Another writer in the same paper countered that the chock-a-block schedule of daily activities meant that 'the first prerequisite of casual liaisons, boredom, is absent'.

Widely suspected within the political class as being 'un-Irish', the new holiday camps were denied proper pub facilities when the Dáil voted down a private member's bill to grant licences in 1949, even though some deputies argued that in the absence of pubs, holiday-makers would hold private 'bottle parties' instead which could degenerate into occasions of sin. The weather that same summer was uncommonly hot and dry, and the low milk yields caused a shortage of milk and ice cream in Dublin city and county. Press reports held the holiday camps partly to blame for snatching milk and ice cream from the lips of ordinary decent citizens.

Visitors to Butlins Mosney, Red Island and the seaside towns north of Dublin were familiar with tradesmen from Northern Ireland hawking Yellowman, a brittle honeycombed toffee made of butter, golden syrup, brown sugar, vinegar and bicarbonate of soda. The ultimate in rough, ready and cheap confectionery, it was generally knocked into saleable chunks with a hammer.

While Yellowman was a summer staple across much of Ireland's northern seaboard, it has always had a special association with the annual Auld Lammas livestock fair in Ballycastle, County Antrim, where it has been linked in song and verse with a snack of dried seaweed called Dulse, which its fans consumed like potato crisps.

ଔ   ଔ   ଔ   ଔ

As tastes became more sophisticated, however, both Dulse and Yellowman gradually fell out of favour with the reporters of *The Irish Times*. A 1954 visitor to the Ballycastle Fair praised Yellowman as 'a strange and wonderful sweetmeat' while another in 1958 recommended the 'famous' toffee.

A day-tripper in 1967 didn't seem pleased that the traditional street fiddlers and ballad singers were now being drowned out by 'a Beatle-sound from loudspeakers projecting from the record shops'. He described Dulse

SWEET MEMORIES

EUGENE MCELDOWNEY, THE 1960s

There is one type of confectionery from my 1960s childhood which I forever associate with salt air, purple heather, green hills and the roar of the sea — Yellowman. It is practically unknown outside of Northern Ireland and even there you can only be sure to find it in Ballycastle in County Antrim.

I had my first encounter with Yellowman as a child on holidays in the Glens of Antrim. I can still recall the joy of biting into a slab of this honey-flavoured toffee and experiencing the burst of sweetness that filled my mouth. And for a child it had one other marvellous attraction — it lasted for a long time. Ten minutes later, I was still chewing on that single piece.

Did you treat your Mary Anne to some dulse and Yellow Man,

At the Ould Lammas Fair in Ballycastle-O?

Ah . . . Yellowman!

and Yellowman as still 'the staples' of the fair, but with equally little sign of enthusiasm for either. He wrote: 'The seaweed has been collected during the month and dried at the rocks at Ballintoy or brought from Donegal. It sells at a shilling for a big handful. Yellowman, a brittle sweet substance, is hammered from large blocks by the stallholders and sold in plastic bags.'

When *The Irish Times* returned in 1977, it was in the person of someone who was clearly having difficulty immersing himself in the holiday spirit. He set out his stall early, claiming: 'Moore Street in Dublin provides a more entertaining daily show than Ballycastle can muster once a year. What Moore Street does not sell, however, are Dulse and Yellowman. Dubliners have been mercifully spared these delicacies which would offend the nostrils of a skunk and upset the stomach of an ostrich. Dulse is merely seaweed gathered on the beach, dried out, and sold at 10p per bag.

'Yellowman tastes even worse. If Hell is as bad as it's reputed to be, Yellowman will be on the menu regularly. A yellow sort of hard substance, no one seemed to know what it was made up of. I myself believe it is a sort of mixture of chalk and sandstone with some additive to give it the bad taste.'

෫ ෫ ෫ ෫

Sponsored Programmes: They Fought for Every Farthing Like Wolves

In the years before 1961, when television started up in Ireland, the sponsored radio shows became woven into the social fabric to an extent that has no counterpart in today's fragmented multimedia world.

The biggest of them all was *The Kennedys of Castleross*, set in a humdrum midlands town based on Mullingar. The twice-weekly soap first aired in 1955 and quickly took a vice-like grip on the public's imagination. Every Tuesday and Thursday at one o'clock offices, factories and farms stopped for tea as the entire nation eavesdropped on the latest gossip from Mrs Kennedy's corner shop.

The same lunch-time slot on other days was coveted by other, more real confectionery companies. Today, Jacob-Fruitfield make biscuits and sweets, including Scots Clan and Silvermints. In the 1950s and 1960s, they were two separate companies that both vied for the one o'clock

spot. On Mondays, Fruitfield filled it with their Fruitfield Information Desk manned by 'Tom' and 'Peggy' who answered listeners' queries on cooking, gardening and other household activities. Meanwhile, Jacob's had two smash hits with *Come Fly With Me*, which flew host Harry Thullier around the world on Aer Lingus to interview celebrities, and *Women's Hour*, an agony aunt show presented by Frankie Byrne.

Thullier also presented *Leisure Time* sponsored by Tayto Crisps, which invited listeners to 'take it easy with Tayto' to the sounds of easy-listening tunes. Brookfield Sweets took a more upbeat approach, featuring a weekly playlist of discs labelled 'slipped', 'snipped', 'flipped' and 'chipped'. A slipped disc was one that had fallen from favour, a snipped one came from a movie soundtrack, a flipped one was a B-side and a chipped one was a golden oldie. Finally, a guest would be asked to pick which record should be 'nipped', or banished forever from the airwaves. The judge would then be sent away with a box of Brookfield sweets for their troubles.

At lunch-time on Fridays, Urney Chocolates sponsored *The Planet Man*, described as 'a spaceship serial running on disc'. The host giving an Irish gloss to the imported sci-fi series was a young Gay Byrne who was treble-jobbing as a radio presenter, a variety show compere and an insurance clerk by day.

Byrne wrote that he had his eye on this 'gorgeous girl with red hair who played the harp and sang' called Kathleen Watkins and he took it for granted she knew who he was. 'In fact,' he later recalled, 'although I myself fancied that the whole nation knew me from the Urney programme, Miss Watkins told me afterwards that she was always running for a bus at the time so she never heard it.' Happily, a matchmaker stepped in and before too long they were engaged.

The young Byrne's cockiness wasn't entirely misplaced, because those who hosted and starred in the sponsored shows were amongst the top celebrities of their day. Such was the clout of these programmes with the Irish public that when the Gateaux Cakes-sponsored soap *The Dalys of Honeydew Farm* went off the air during a strike, it was reported that sales of all cakes went into a nationwide slump.

By the late 1950s, sponsored programmes were the most important revenue stream to Radio Éireann after the licence fee. It hadn't always been so, and when the state broadcaster started up as 2RN in the 1920s advertising was barely tolerated as a necessary evil. Adverts for foreign products were especially frowned upon, and in order to discourage them the broadcaster charged £10 per five-minute slot to foreign companies, which was double the rate for native firms.

The short soundbite adverts we know today were still decades in the future and the earliest ads were five minutes in length and took the form of what the government described as 'lectures advertising particular Irish industries or national concerns or undertakings'. With time, these shows stretched to fifteen or thirty minutes. An early sponsor of the extended format shows was the Dublin firm of Williams & Woods who made a range of affordable sweets including the bestselling macaroons and aniseed balls, simplified by the children of Ireland to 'Nancy balls'.

In an era when firms like Fry's were better known for their cocoa drinks than their chocolate, one of the very first to jump on the radio bandwagon was the Savoy Cocoa Company which sponsored *The Savoy Minstrels*, exposing Irish listeners to the latest sounds of black America, even if the crooners on the discs were usually white.

The majority of Ireland's political masters detested and despised jazz, which they often referred to as 'race music'. Throughout the 1930s, politicians and radio bosses tried to browbeat advertisers into sponsoring shows featuring Irish classical and traditional musicians. The response of the advertisers was invariably that the listeners wanted crooners and jazz, and that was what they would have.

The advent of the Second World War destroyed the advertising industry in Ireland, and Radio Éireann took advantage to finally try to force jazz off the air. *The Irish Times* reported: 'An official "taboo" has been placed on dance music at Radio Éireann. The brake has been applied gradually and the small number of dance music records broadcast recently will be the last to be enjoyed by licence-holders. It is understood, however, that the term 'dance music' will be roughly interpreted as standing for 'swing', 'jive', 'hot' music, or music with a vocal chorus sung by a crooner. Broadcasts of continental dance music, much of which lies outside these classifications, will probably be continued.'

Shortly after the ban was imposed, Labour's Dick Corish praised the 'improvement' in the service, saying that if the Irish people had been subjected to 'crooning and jazzing' for too much longer 'we would have had very little music in this country within the next generation'.

By the time the early 1950s came around, Fry-Cadbury were sponsoring a lunch-time music show that is best described as pale and uninteresting. The musical fare was provided by the popular English bandleader Billy Tenant whose signature tune was 'Calling All The Workers', but it was only when Tenant's shoes were filled by *The Kennedys of Castleross* that all the workers really did answer the call to down tools and boil up the kettle.

In the opening action of the very first episode of *The Kennedys*, the widowed Mrs Kennedy must disappoint a regular customer, Mrs Shaw, who is on the phone looking to have some sweets delivered to her door. Mrs Kennedy assures her that the sweets will be dispatched once her youngest son, who doubles as her delivery boy, arrives home from football practice.

The young Hugh Leonard, later to become a distinguished dramatist, was an early recruit to write scripts for the hefty sum of eight guineas per episode, which was almost as much as his weekly pay packet from his day job as a civil servant.

For the writers, there were certain ground rules that had to be followed. The prime directive was that Mrs Kennedy must always be at the centre of the parallel universe that was Castleross. After her, for no apparent reason, an old loafer called Peadar had to be given a few lines to say at least once a week.

In all, there were more than a dozen characters, but cash was tight and the writers were limited to using no more than four, Mrs Kennedy included, in any given instalment. Leonard later recalled: 'On certain rare occasions, the reading of a will, a wedding day, or the eruption of Mount Bejaysus, I could go mad and employ a fourth actor.'

Marie Kean who played Mrs Kennedy earned a paltry two guineas per show. The going rate for the other actors was a mere thirty shillings but, in the words of Hugh Leonard: 'They fought for every farthing of it like wolves.' As the scriptwriter, he would have to decide who'd earn a few bob for a bit part in any given week, and who wouldn't. This didn't win him many friends amongst the cast of stand-bys. He remarked: 'The actors thought I hated them. Too bloody true.'

Over the course of time, batty characters, like Birdie O'Hanlon (catchphrase 'Birdie must fly'), and plain bad ones, like the gombeen Jim Lonergan, became like extended family members to countless devoted listeners. Actress Marie Kean became used to receiving fan mail addressed to 'Mrs Kennedy'. When President John F. Kennedy visited Ireland in 1963 he was reportedly asked in all innocence: 'Are you related to the Kennedys of Castleross?'

Ever the consummate statesman, the leader of the free world replied that he was indeed.

As the years rolled by in an Ireland where change came slowly, the show settled into a snoozy comfort zone where, according to Leonard, 'no dilemma was too piddling, no outcome too banal, no sentiment too trite to take centre stage'.

The happenings in Castleross may have been piddling and banal, but that was how the listeners liked it. On one occasion, Hugh Leonard gave the moany Peadar a throwaway line about the low butter yield of Friesian cattle. The response was a sack full of letters from dairy farmers complaining that Peadar was damaging their trade by casting a slur on their livestock.

The writer got a dressing down from the advertising agency behind the show, insisting that sponsors Fry-Cadbury would not want to alienate any part of the farming community. The wrong was quickly righted, with Peadar announcing in a follow-up episode that he'd been entirely mistaken about Friesians.

If the farmers had a cow about Peadar's misplaced comments, the entire listening population seemed up in arms when Leonard had the feckless bad taste to bring up the subject of childbirth at the nation's dinner tables.

The writer decided to gift Castleross housewife Pat with a new baby. The first signpost as to where the plot was going came when the local doctor called in Pat's husband Brian for a chat about possible complications with the birth.

The programme aired and all hell broke loose. RTÉ was swamped with letters protesting at this gross act of indecency. One complaint was signed by every member of a family, including a smudge from a year-old infant. Another woman fumed that she'd been embarrassed into making her eighteen-year-old son leave the room.

The problem for the sponsors was that a number of episodes dealing with Pat's complicated birth were already in the can, and Hugh Leonard refused to write new ones. Sticking to their motto that the listener is always right, the show's makers snipped out all references to the touchy subject. The pre-recorded shows were now shorter, but the missing minutes were easily filled in with a little light music.

The upshot was that sensitive listeners were spared even the slightest grisly detail, and the next anyone heard of the matter after Brian's chat with the doctor was when someone said, 'Hello, Pat. How's the new baby?'

The final correspondence Leonard received on the matter caused him some amusement. It congratulated him for delivering the new cast member with such sensitivity, complimenting him, 'You would hardly know she'd had it.'

Shortly after Teilifís Éireann opened on the last day of 1961, Fry-Cadbury shocked the nation with the announcement that they were ending their sponsorship of *The Kennedys* and diverting their broadcasting budget into the new medium of television. A Cadbury's executive explained that the switch was a no-brainer because: 'The visual impulse to buy is a key part of selling confectionery. *The Kennedys of Castleross* couldn't provide that, TV could.'

This makes more sense than the rumour doing the rounds at the time which claimed that Fry's, who were in the business of selling cocoa, got tired of Mrs Kennedy trying to foist 'a nice cup of tea' on her visitors.

When push came to shove, RTÉ decided that its top radio show must be saved, and the station put its own money into *The Kennedys*. However, *The Dalys of Honeybrook Farm* wasn't so lucky when Gateaux announced it was to be replaced with a much cheaper pop show. *The Irish Times* lamented the decision, saying that 'the listening public have become addicted' over its lengthy run, and hoping the broadcaster would take 'the same motherly and auspicious attitude' to *The Dalys* as it had to *The Kennedys*. It wasn't to be.

No show in the history of Irish radio, before or since, has become so much a part of people's lives as *The Kennedys of Castleross*. But as it reached its eighteenth year in 1973, it remained steadfastly stuck in a state of arrested development in the 1950s. An Ireland which had outgrown *Castleross* marked its passing, but had no misgivings about letting go.

In the show's heyday, a stray comment sparked a sack full of protest letters; when RTÉ announced it was pulling the plug, it received just one.

Lent: Fast, Abstinence and, Finally, Easter Eggs

'Giving up sweets for Lent' was a phrase dreaded by generations of Irish Catholic children, for whom the forty days of self-denial from Ash Wednesday to Easter Sunday represented an eternity of cruel and unusual punishment.

Each year, just as a stretch was beginning to brighten the evenings, the Catholic bishops would read out their Lenten Regulations from the pulpit, and every newspaper would give them high priority.

The regulations unveiled by Dublin's Archbishop John Charles McQuaid in February 1959 give a flavour of the times. He expected nothing less from his flock than solemn obedience.

Before coming to the dietary stuff, the archbishop

gave a rap on the knuckles to all those 'heedless' parents 'who, abandoning the authority they hold in sacred trust from God, neglect to control firmly the leisure time of their children'. He expanded: 'In particular we deplore the unseeing negligence of some parents who permit immature boys and girls to be exposed to the dangerous occasions of sin provided by certain teenage dances.'

Shortly after, Archbishop McQuaid challenged Ireland's doctors and psychologists to come up with a distinctly Irish way of teaching teens about the birds and bees, without telling them too much. He reminded them that they had a duty 'to supply instruction in chastity that is accurate, clear, adequate and supernatural' in such a manner to 'tranquilise the adolescent'.

The Lenten Regulations for 1959 demanded that all Catholics should offer up their penance of giving up things, for all those 'suffering persecution for the faith, especially in Communist China'. The regulations added that no Catholic should have anything to do with any Communist sympathiser and their 'perverse way of life'.

The regulations dictated that Catholics aged between twenty-one and sixty were bound by the laws of fast and abstinence. Fasting meant eating just one meal a day, with an optional light morning and evening snack for the weak-willed. Abstinence meant no meat. Those between the ages of seven and twenty-one were bound only by the law of abstinence. During the season of Lent 1959, every day was a fast day except Sundays and St Patrick's Day.

While children under seven were exempt under Church law, and older kids were only obliged to give up meat, the culture of the time dictated that every Catholic child should give up sweets and chocolate for the duration.

Most sweetshops of the time had at least one collection

box on the counter bearing the slogan 'Penny For The Black Babies', and these filled up over the course of Lent.

The upshot was that Ireland's sweetshop owners looked forward to Lent with even more trepidation than did the nation's children. The Lenten Regulations were lifted for St Patrick's Day, and each 17 March, the sweet sellers seized on the holiday as brief window of cash flow.

The confectioners' trade magazine advised: 'As confectionery events go, St Patrick's Day does not rank with the importance of Easter. March 17th does, however, make a good "filler" display. St Patrick's Day should be given the monopoly of one show window, wherein green and confections and Irish novelties and favours should be presented amid appropriate surroundings.'

Speaking in 2011, Eddie Kavanagh of Kavanagh's sweetshop on Dublin's Aungier Street, reported: 'St Patrick's Day is always a comical day in the shop because we get customers coming in with their children on that

SWEET MEMORIES
DEIRDRE PURCELL, THE 1950s

You are eight years old and, at long last, it is Saturday. Pocket money day.

But first comes the sweeping of the lino in the dining room, sitting room and hall, plus the concrete floor of the kitchen/scullery. Then the dusting. The mahogany hall stand. The ship's piano. The clock on the sitting-room mantelpiece. Then, on hands and knees, the back-breaking application of Mansion Polish to the red quarry tiles of the porch, followed by their buffing with a succession of cloths. Then Brasso-ing the front-door knocker. Then the claim for sixpence.

You call for Alice who lives across the road and ignore the shouts and waving fists of car drivers on the main road as, chatting and planning, you weave across the main road: two gobstoppers, six Honey Bees or ten Nancy balls for the first penny? A bag of broken biscuits for twopence?

The shop is a cave of sugary delight. 'How many of them for a penny, Mister?' pointing to the Honey Bees.

'Six, love,' with a faint sigh. 'I told you that last week. And the week before. And the week before that.'

A consultation with Alice. 'All right, you buy a packet of sweet cigarettes and two fizzbags and I'll buy a penny's worth of Honey Bees and bon bons and we'll share?'

'No. I don't want cigarettes,' she rebels. 'I hate them. Anyway, I want to buy satin cushions and bon bons . . .'

'Girls, girls!' The shopkeeper intervenes.

You ignore him. 'All right. You buy six bon bons Alice, and one fizzbag and two gobstoppers,' I have my negotiating hat on, 'and the cushions, and I'll buy cigarettes and four liquorice strings, ten Nancy balls and a bag of broken biscuits that we can share. And you can give me one gobstopper and a lick of your fizzbag.'

'I want to buy the broken biscuits. Anytime we share, you always take the biggest bits.'

'I won't take the biggest bits this time. I promise!'

It's touch-and-go as negotiations sway this way and that, but, eventually, to the obvious relief of the shopkeeper, we settle on the dibs, but watch him carefully as he counts our order into paper bags.

Already munching, we stroll back to our road through the honking, maddened drivers, just avoiding a dig from the snub, smelly nose of a double-decker bus. You're content. You have a penny left and she doesn't.

day. It's a tradition for a lot of them, because as kids they used to come into the shop for sweets.

'The St Patrick's Day parade used to go down Aungier Street for many years. The same families would congregate outside the shop, get their sweets, watching the parade. Now the parade goes down Dame Street but after the parade, those children from my youth come up to the shop with their kids and they want to show the kids the sweets they had when they were children.'

In general, however, the only good thing about Lent from the sweet seller's point of view was that it acted as a countdown to the bonanza that was Easter.

An advert from 1902 placed by Lemon & Co. of Dublin's Sackville Street (now O'Connell Street) advertised a range of 'perfectly pure' Easter eggs described as: 'Sugar, Chocolate, Wooden, Marzipan, Hand-painted Satin Eggs, Ducks, Chickens, Cocks, Hens and all sorts of Easter gifts filled with sweets.'

Another from 1894 advertised 'the largest variety in Ireland' with 'prices from one halfpenny to fifteen shillings each'. Fifteen shillings for a confectionery egg was an enormous sum at a time when the vast majority of Irish children would have been thrilled to wake to a real duck or goose egg wrapped in a scrap of ribbon on Easter Sunday.

The confectionery Easter egg reflects the ancient association of spring with eggs, and it was only at the start of the twentieth century that chocolate began to displace the much older marzipan, toffee and sugar eggs decorated with icing. One Italian account from 1820 reported: 'They are usually filled with imitations of all sorts of fruits. In Paris, they put in a number of nick-nacks, little almanacs, smelling bottles with essences, and even things of value as presents.'

By the start of the 1960s chocolate Easter eggs had

virtually wiped out the competition and, with Irish factories lagging decades behind the latest production techniques, Cadbury's two Dublin plants alone employed almost 3,000 workers making Easter eggs by hand.

In 1963, the Second Vatican Council began doing for the Catholic Church what The Beatles had just begun doing for youth culture. A Church defined along hard lines from time immemorial suddenly began to mellow out and the forces of social change, ice bound for decades, began to thaw.

One of the first Catholic leaders to see the straws in the wind was the Bishop of Derry and Raphoe, Dr Charles Tyndall, who reached out to bring popular culture into the embrace of traditional Church teaching. As the Weight Watchers organisation was launching in 1963, Bishop Tyndall declared in his Lenten pastoral letter: 'I don't think it is irrelevant or wrong to say we can slim for Jesus Christ. That is simply another way of expressing the spiritual meaning of abstinence.'

In the short four years since Archbishop McQuaid had laid down the law on what and when Irish Catholics could eat during Lent, the country had enjoyed a spurt of prosperity, and Bishop Tyndall now expressed concern that the idea of self-denial had suddenly become 'unpopular'. He urged his flock to 'review' their 'animal appetites' and cut down on chocolates, butter, sugar, jam, cigarettes and beer.

The Second Vatican Council wrapped up in December 1965 and Lent in Ireland would never be quite the same again. It's safe to suspect that when Archbishop McQuaid read out the new Lenten Regulations in February 1966, he did so with a heavy heart.

In 1959 every day of Lent, bar Sundays and St Patrick's Day, was a day of fast and abstinence. From 1966 onwards, this was slashed to just two, Ash Wednesday and Good Friday. He stressed: 'This relaxation of the Lenten fast ought to stimulate the faithful to give more generous alms.'

For the children of Ireland, the archbishop had even better news. Under the old rules, everyone between the ages of seven and twenty-one was obliged to give up things. Under the new rules, all kids under the age of fifteen were free to give up as little or as much as they liked.

Many Irish children to this day try to give up sweets for Lent, but if Archbishop McQuaid were still around, he would surely argue that 1966 was when the rot set in.

CHAPTER FIVE

1960S SWEETSHOPS, BUS STOPS AND STAR TREK GUM

At the start of the 1960s, the Irish people went on a sweet-eating binge. With the economy entering a mini-boom, a small prosperity and a curious feel-good factor settled over the land. In 1961, the average Irish person was eating some 160 grams of confectionery each week. By 1965, this had shot up to 200 grams.

The traditional local sweetshop thrived, although usually now in the guise of an outlet known in the trade as a CTN, or confectioner/tobacconist/newsagent. In rural Ireland especially, sweetshop owners continued to wield plenty of clout as pillars of their communities.

Dublin was expanding fast into the surrounding countryside, and the capital's planners were acutely aware of the need to keep on sweet terms with the confectioners.

The Irish Times reported in 1963 that it wasn't so long since 'the shopkeepers in Dublin were feared so much by the local authority that the task of selecting bus stop sites, and putting the appropriate markings on the road, was solemnly left to CIÉ, even though it is not the statutory body to appoint stopping places or mark public roads'.

Criticising the gombeen parish pump politics which had left the country's roads and public transport in a mess, the writer complained: 'An irate sweetshop owner, annoyed at having a bus stop moved from outside his door, is to be feared and respected more than the public inconvenienced, and perhaps endangered by, its illogical situation.'

The sweetshop owners didn't like change of any sort, but it was coming.

In the early 1960s, the big confectionery manufacturers sent out teams of young merchandisers whose job it was to persuade the sweet sellers that the fancy window display was ancient history. The new idea spreading from the United States was that customers came in to a shop for 'destination' items, namely their cigarettes or newspaper. When they'd reached their destination they'd buy sweets, chocolate or ice cream if the impulse hit them.

The job of the new merchandising men was to talk the shopkeepers into rearranging their shops, taking the sweets out of the window and placing them on the counter where they were within arm's reach for that impulse buy. The new message was: 'Let the whole shop be your window.'

At the same time, the sweetshop owners were fighting a rearguard action against the packaging of sweets which interfered with their traditional practice of weighing out short measures on their counter scales. The hygiene message that the government had been trying to hammer home since the start of the 1950s was beginning to get through, helped by the fact that more customers were opting for pre-packaged sweets and snacks. This changeover was hastened by the fact that the wrapped candy bar was beginning to replace the traditional apple or sandwich as an acceptable mid-morning or afternoon snack.

For decades, sweetshop owners, who were well in with the manufacturers, were supplied with large boxes of broken biscuits and chocolate bars, with brittle Kit-Kat leading the way. These cut-price factory rejects were big favourites with school kids, and most of the shops favoured with a steady supply happened to be located close to schools. By the close of the decade, however, broken biscuits and bars were vanishing from the stores. This was partly because improved technology meant there were fewer broken biscuits, and partly because the manufacturers decided it made little sense to undercut their own expensively packaged new lines with cheap cast-offs that tasted just as good for half the pocket money.

But while big changes were in the air for confectionery sellers, the working conditions for the thousands employed in Ireland's confectionery factories had changed little since the 1920s and 1930s when many of the plants first opened. The vast majority of confectionery workers were women, who, by law, could be paid roughly half what a man would receive for a similar job. Visitors to several factories remarked that the toilet and washroom facilities left an awful lot to be desired. Usually, this was the fault of feckless employers, but sometimes the staff were equally to blame. A circular to HB's female ice cream workforce in 1965 complained that 'portions of ice cream have been thrown on the floors of the toilets and cloakroom'. They were ordered to clean up their act or suffer the consequences.

The same stern notice from management stressed that each girl must put in a full forty-two-and-a-half hours per week at their work station, clocking in by 8.04 a.m. and not moving from that spot without permission of a supervisor. Anyone clocking in between 8.04 a.m. and 8.10 a.m. would be allowed to work, but would be docked one hour's pay. Anyone arriving after that would be sent home and readmitted at 2 p.m. at a loss of five hours' pay. Nail varnish, hair rollers and jewellery were all forbidden, but wedding rings could be kept on.

At the end of a long list of dos and don'ts, each girl was reminded to 'put her house in order' or sterner discipline would be imposed.

SWEET MEMORIES
PAUL WOODFULL, THE 1960s

The best sweets I recall as a child in the 1960s were Gifties, Pink Panther bars and Candy Cigarettes. The worst were probably the racist Golly bar, Zubes — which a friend of mine used to buy so he wouldn't have to share them — and, of course, the ones you were invited to rummage for in a Catholic priest's pocket.

1960s Assortment

Ice Cream Van-dalism

The ice cream on a stick was a new sensation that swept Ireland in the 1960s. The idea had been around since the 1930s when an American seller reputedly watched a young customer struggle to choose between an ice cream sandwich and a chocolate bar. The enterprising ice cream man came up with an ingenious solution by covering an ice cream bar with chocolate, mounting it on a stick, and calling it his I-Scream-Bar.

The new invention took some time to catch on in Ireland, probably because the factories were well behind the times and the machinery wasn't in place. When HB launched its choc ice in 1948 it was along the lines of the I-Scream-Bar but without the stick.

In the summer of 1960, HB launched its Choc Stik with an ad campaign emphasising the convenience of the stick. The Choc Stik was a big hit and HB quickly followed up with its first Ice Pop, Brunch and

Super Split. Across town from HB in Rathfarnham, Merville Ices in Finglas invited the press to see their latest machines for injecting fruit syrup into ice cream to create their latest ripple flavour. One reporter noted that ice creams on sticks were grabbing market share from the established tubs, wafers and bricks. He wrote: 'Ice cream on sticks seems a clean, sensible idea. It should do away with a lot of sticky fingers and messed clothes.'

Ice cream sales also received a big boost in the 1960s with the arrival in force of the ice cream van with its out-of-tune chimes driving parents and children to distraction, although for different reasons. In Belfast, Alderman Gerry Fitt branded these newcomers as dangerous 'pied pipers', luring children to run excitedly onto busy roadways. Speaking shortly after a child had died, Fitt said that if ice cream vans were to be tolerated, every driver should have a helper who would guard the children while they milled about.

In Derry, the corporation went further and banned vans from playing their chimes between 9 a.m. and 7 p.m. in order to stop stampedes of pupils during school lunch-times and at going-home time. In Dublin, the city fathers summonsed a number of van vendors under various bye-laws, only for the judge to throw out the cases. The authorities did manage to impose a ban on chimes at some beauty spots, but this did nothing to harm business, much to the annoyance of those who resented the invasion of the countryside by both the ice

Damian Corless

SWEET MEMORIES
KIERAN CONNOLLY, THE 1960s

I had an idyllic 1960s childhood. My parents migrated to Dublin from the midlands when I was a baby and I would spend the school year as a 'Jackeen' on the streets of Inchicore. During the summer holidays, I was a 'culchie' moving between my grandmothers' small farms in the rolling hills outside Moate. In Dublin, I served mass in the Oblates, where a full-size replica of the Lourdes Grotto dominated the church grounds, and where each year thousands gathered for the annual torchlight procession. In Westmeath, I helped milk cows, save hay and catch monstrous sods of wet turf thrown to me (or at me) by my dad and various uncles.

In this double-life, Emeralds were my country sweets. My maternal grandmother was a tiny, wiry woman who produced ten children and who passed away peacefully in her ninety-third year. She continued to work her vegetable plot of rich, dark clay well into her late eighties, this despite smoking all her life. But she had another vice aside from cigarettes: Emeralds.

As soon as I could prove to her that I was able to cycle her

monstrous *Raleigh High Nelly* up and down the *boreen*, she entrusted me with the trip to the shop/pub in Castledaly for the messages. Her list always included a packet of Emeralds. When I returned with the still intact packet, I would be allocated my fair share and sent outside to play.

In my memory, the sun always shone in that magical place. Fields were surrounded by thick mysterious hedges, full of hideouts and dappled shade. The breeze was always warm. When I am jaded and stressed, I seek out my 'happy place' and that is it. But nothing triggers it as effectively as an Emerald melting in my mouth. The nuttiness, the toffee-ness, the chewiness and the chocolatey-ness transport me to those balmy afternoons with the sights, sounds, smells and taste of my childhood.

Iced caramels were my Dublin sweet, and remain equally effective as a memory trigger. I bought mine in Mr Ward's sweetshop on Tyrconnell Road on my way to various events in the Oblate church.

In the late 1960s, everything seemed to revolve around that magnificent building. It was packed every Sunday, with volunteer ushers on standby to move anyone fainting from the oven-like heat. Every ceremony attracted the same tremendous support from the local population but none more so that the annual torchlight procession in February each year. Carrying a torch, which was a candle surrounded by a paper shape was a tricky enough business and required a certain level of concentration. Alex Ferguson chews on wads of chewing gum to help him focus, but an altar boy would be excommunicated for that deed so I would drop in to Mr Ward's beforehand. The most luxurious sweet then (and now) was iced caramels.

Stocked up with a supply, I could easily make them last the hour or so it took to meander around the Oblate church grounds at the head of the vast singing, swaying, murmuring throng.

Iced caramels were for one thing only and that was chewing – after a few seconds savouring the sweet, granite hard exterior you had to crack through to the soft interior. The standard sweet had a centre layer of medium-hard chewable toffee surrounded by a softer almost fudge-like toffee (not like the hard brittle toffee of a Flash bar mind). The best ones were missing the hard centre, you might get two or three of those in a packet.

The amazing thing about both Emeralds and iced caramels is that they taste exactly the same today. Even the smell as you unwrap them is the very same. Mr Ward and my granny have long gone to the great sweetshop in the sky, where you no doubt can still get Peggy's legs and Urney's Rovals (my dad worked in Urney's of Tallaght for a time – how lucky was I?) and four different flavours of Club milks. But I am content in the knowledge that today I can stroll into almost any petrol station, spend a few euro, and with the help of my Emeralds and iced caramels bring those idyllic days to life again.

cream vendors and the great unwashed who gave them custom.

One griped in 1964: 'Have you been up the Dublin Mountains recently of a weekend? A few years ago you could drive the family up Glencree and around the Pine Forest country and you could be pardoned for being annoyed if you met two dozen cars of an afternoon. Last Sunday, the roadsides were jammed with cars and it is as hard to get parking space as if it were O'Connell Street on a busy weekday. A sign of the times is that the mobile ice cream vans are now finding it very profitable indeed to 'go up the mountains' at weekends where, without any jingles to advertise their presence, they do enough business to make the operation profitable.'

The same complainant muttered that the new mass ownership of cars had ruined Ireland's beaches with 'the shrilling of children and screeching of transistorised Beatles'. Another agreed, saying that proud car owners were turning the north Dublin resort of Skerries into a honky-tonk of 'gaudy multicoloured kiosks with their jukeboxes, coffee dispensers, slot machines and an abundance of litter'. Once again 'the chiming ice cream van plying its wares will benefit' from this vandalism.

The Poor Mouth

With the growing prosperity of the 1960s, the people of Ireland had a little extra spare change in their pockets and many chose to spend it on sweets. But even before the binge began, the nation's teeth had already been in a shocking state of disrepair.

A few years earlier, a top dentist had told the press: 'If all sweetshops were prohibited by law then the dental surgeon's work with children would largely disappear.'

This was never going to happen, of course, but, in

1962, the Minister for Health Seán MacEntee had his mind set on taking some remedial action. To confirm that the dental decay was as bad as he feared, he ordered a survey of 27,000 children. It established that in Dublin and Cork the average ten-year-old had six teeth missing, decayed or filled. Worse, Irish teenagers had to negotiate their crucial snogging years with one third of their teeth blighted or gone. However, the survey singled out one glistening oasis of fresh breath confidence.

In the village of Patrickswell in County Limerick, the report said: 'Fluorine is naturally present in the public water supply. In this village, the children's teeth were markedly healthier than elsewhere.'

Legislation approving the fluoridation of water supplies had been passed in 1961 but a body calling itself the Pure Water Association had stirred up an effective poisoned-well scare. The Pure Water lobby charged that fluoridation amounted to an unwarranted 'mass medication' capable of producing untold horrors.

Pushing ahead with his scheme to fluoridate the country's drinking water, Minister MacEntee put it on the record that there were only two possible alternatives to his plan, and that both were clearly impossible. One would be to treble the number of dentists in the state to 1,800 at huge cost. Apart from the expense, it would take years to train 1,200 extra dentists. Especially with the country's 600 existing practitioners fighting tooth and drill to preserve their closed shop.

The other alternative to fluoridation would be to improve people's eating habits and dental hygiene. The Irish were now rivalling their British neighbours as the biggest sweet eaters in the world, and mountainous dollops of refined sugar were stirred into tea, porridge and anything else that would bear sweetening. Toothbrush sales were dismal.

The minister ruled out getting people to take better care of their teeth. In his view, the Irish poor mouth was an inevitable by-product of progress. As the pamphlet explained: 'The fundamental cause of bad teeth is the modern diet – and this is something that cannot be changed substantially. Ireland is no exception here: all advanced countries must pay the penalties of the modern dietary and none has found a way of changing either the diet or the habits of eating, least of all among the children.'

Richie Ryan TD was an impassioned champion of Pure Water. The minister's report, charged Ryan, was an unscrupulous effort 'to push fluoridated water down the throats of an unsuspecting public'. Ryan went so far as to argue that fluoride might actually cause teeth to rot, claiming: 'Adults in a fluoridated area have many more decayed, missing or filled teeth than their counterparts in a non-fluoridated area.'

Dublin Corporation debated whether to accept the will of the government and fluoridate the capital's drinking water. When the vote was called, Richie Ryan howled at those about to vote in favour that they would 'be counted with the murderers of the children of Dublin'.

His impassioned cry was to no avail. The fluoridation measure was passed by a margin of twenty-five votes to fifteen. Dubliners' teeth began to improve dramatically despite a sharp rise in sweet eating, while water-related deaths remained largely confined to drownings.

The Chocolate Bars are Getting Smaller: The Coming of the Supermarket

As a very young child, I was early through the doors when Ireland's first proper supermarket opened in Finglas village in 1965. It was called Quinn's, not yet Superquinn, and its glamour drew the crowds.

Converted from a cinema, it was a maze of aisles you could get lost in, stacked with varieties of produce never before gathered in one place, and a ceiling so high you could fly a kite. A few years later, with plenty of time to stare as a teenage shelf-stacker and bag-packer, I realised that it wasn't one but two ceilings, with an ugly join where two big spaces had been knocked together.

But when Ireland's first supermarket opened, no one minded the join, because it was so much bigger, better, cleaner and cheaper than anything else around.

Shopping before supermarkets required patience and planning. Filling the shopping bag might involve popping into the grocer, greengrocer, newsagent, butcher, fishmonger, haberdasher, chemist and off-licence.

Many items were shelved behind a broad counter and you had to point and ask for what you wanted. Cash registers were rare, sliding wooden drawers common. A receipt would consist of totted sums on a scrap of brown wrapping paper.

Hygiene was low priority. An order of ham, corned beef and cheese could be sliced together with no pretence to wipe the machine, often in a mist of cigarette smoke.

There was none of that 'customer is king' rot. The shopkeeper was king, and demanded respect. And woe betide anyone who antagonised their local grocer if the next one was half-a-mile up the road.

No sooner had Feargal Quinn stepped in to sweep away the old order than he was joined by Leitrim-born Pat Quinn, recently returned from Canada. In 1966, Pat opened his first Quinnsworth store in Stillorgan and a famous rivalry began.

The pair seemed polar opposites. Feargal was soft-spoken and methodical; Pat the brashest motor mouth Irish business had ever seen. Pat had grown up in the family pub/grocery. In Canada, he grew a grocery

---

Damian Corless

business by day, while, by night, he promoted shows by The Rolling Stones, The Beach Boys, Johnny Cash, Roy Orbison and The Supremes.

Pat's first Quinnsworth was, for the times, a freak show. Perched in a booth like a demented motorsport commentator, he'd bark out news of special offers and great cash giveaways over the speaker system.

There was more than a touch of David Brent from *The Office* in Pat, the businessman who craved acclaim as a star of comedy. He pushed himself forward at every opportunity. He bought airtime on RTÉ radio for a Quinnsworth-sponsored comedy series starring himself, along with the comic Hal Roche. The other two cast members were directors of the advertising agency that booked the slot.

Cutting a dash around town in his silver Rolls Royce, he became a regular on *The Late Late Show* and at glitterati bashes. Learning that George Best was to get £1,000 to open his newest store, he protested that he was famous enough for the job. The fee went to charity and Georgie stayed in Manchester.

From the get-go Pat went for the 'pile-'em-high, sell-'em-cheap' pitch, coining the term 'yellow pack' for his range of no-frills generic goods.

Feargal, in contrast, was less clear about what he should be selling. When Finglas opened, it sold bras, knickers and even carpets alongside the groceries. Outside, future Formula 1 boss Eddie Jordan provided competition, flogging carpets from a van.

What Feargal Quinn and Pat Quinn had in common was that they changed the way Irish shoppers bought things, including their sweets. Before the coming of the big supermarket, a parent with a kid (or kids) in tow shopping for meat would go to the butchers, or they would go to the vegetable shop for greens. In either place, there was never any prospect that they'd end up having a stand-off over sweets.

But there was no way of escaping the new one-stop supermarkets without having to negotiate the rows of sweets, chocolate bars and lollipops stacked in front of each till. And with the supermarkets came another American brainwave for selling more sweets to more people – bigger bars split into more squares and, later, the family bite-size pack.

The confectionery industry in the States had hired the sales guru Dr Ernest Dichter to help them boost sales. Dichter is credited with dreaming up the term 'focus group' and the ESSO slogan 'Put A Tiger In Your Tank'. At a time when low-calorie sugar drinks were getting a heavy marketing push in the States for the first time, Dichter identified guilt as standing between the shopper and the sweets on display.

To combat this guilt, Dichter came up with the concept of 'self-indulgence in moderation'. He reasoned: 'You will be providing the excuse the customer needs to buy a bar of candy – "After all, I don't have to eat all of it, just a bite and then put the rest away." Seriously, we doubt whether the rest will be put away. However, the consumer will be left with the feeling that candy manufacturers understand him and the bite-size pieces will give him the 'permission' he needs to buy the candy because the manufacturers are going to 'permit' him to eat in moderation.'

The advent of the supermarkets coincided with the signing of a new Anglo-Irish Trade Agreement in 1965 which led to a flood of new sweets onto the Irish market. The agreement came about after the French blackballed Ireland and Britain from joining the European Economic Community (EEC) in 1963. The Dublin government saw the need to shed Ireland's protective wall of import duties in readiness for another attempt to join the Common Market.

The new supermarkets were now free to stock up on sweets and bars that Irish viewers had seen advertised on British channels for years but which had been kept out by high import duties.

Speaking in the Dáil in 1968, the Labour TD Michael O'Leary complained that the supermarkets were using imported sweets and biscuits to draw in customers, while the money spent was now leaving the country.

He charged: 'Up and down the country there are neon signs, and supermarkets which . . . have their own interests in mind first. They push their own business interests, they push their own manufacturers and their own British wholesalers. Only last week, I ventured into one of those commercial temples. I noticed they were pushing British biscuits, British cheese, British confectionery, and so on.'

A short time earlier, the Dáil had debated another worrying new trend in confectionery – chocolate bars were getting smaller. Labour's Dr John O'Connell asked George Colley, the Minister for Industry and Commerce, if he was aware 'that many manufacturers, as well as increasing the price, are reducing the size of the product'.

The minister agreed that this was happening, and there was nothing he could do about it. The 1960s over-the-counter culture had arrived, and the times they were a-changing.

Ice Cream Cold Wars

One of the star turns of the 1960 St Patrick's Day parade through Dublin was the HB ice cream float which featured a rocket ship to depict the space race that was hotting up between the United States and the Soviet

Union. The race was also on in the Cold War between HB and its rivals Merville, Lucan and Palm Grove for control of the growing ice cream and ice pop trade.

Declaring 1961 the Year of the Pop, HB launched its first ice pop on a stick, the HB Pop. By now, however, Palm Grove had stolen a long lead on its rivals in the ice-pop stakes. At a fraction the price of an ice cream, ice pops had won over the young end of the market. Emboldened by this success, Palm Grove was now refusing to supply its in-demand ice pops to shopkeepers unless they agreed to sell Palm Grove ice cream too.

The intense rivalry between HB and Dublin Dairies for the ice cream market in the capital was given an extra edge when HB discovered that Dublin Dairies were passing off HB's famous ice cream cakes as their own.

In their book *The Story of HB*, Paul Mulhern and Kieran Fagan outlined how the HB ice cream cake was the crowning glory of every children's party in the capital from the 1950s through to the 1970s. The proud parents would order the cake in advance, giving the name and age of the child to be spelled out in icing on the top.

Dublin Dairies didn't have the facilities to make ice cream cakes, but they wanted a slice of the business, so they placed a weekly order for un-iced cakes and added a script ordered by their own customers. The HB cakes were then packaged in Dublin Dairies wrappings and the customer was none the wiser.

Of course, it wasn't long before someone at HB twigged what was going on, and HB staff began inserting a round cardboard disc imprinted with the HB logo on the bottom of the cake. The idea was that Dublin Dairies wouldn't see the disc, but the customer would as the slices disappeared.

SWEET MEMORIES
DERMOT BOLGER, THE 1970s

Every childhood should have one golden summer. In 1972, I left primary school early to work as a van-boy (underage) delivering Palm Grove ice cream to shops along the necklace of seaside towns straddling north Dublin's coastline. We may not have supplied nectar from the Gods, but in that blazing sunshine with our bigger rivals HB on strike, shopkeepers flocked around us like we were a relief convoy.

Van drivers were a nomadic race, stopping to swap contraband and compare notes on which shopkeepers were the sharpest to deal with. The sun shone as we parked in lay-bys for lunch. Like sea gulls homing in, other delivery vans would park behind us, with drivers engaged in a brisk, illicit exchange. We were normally divested of around a dozen choc ices and found ourselves in possession of crisps, soft drinks, hot dogs, plastic sunglasses and — on one occasion — two goldfish in a plastic bag that we left dangling on a tree outside a national school for children to find. It was freedom, it was bliss.

HB's executives were exceedingly pleased with themselves for turning the tables on rivals trying to pull a fast one, but they shouldn't have been. Shortly after HB began inserting their discs, a staffer at Dublin Diaries brought one home for his child's party and discovered the ruse. From the following Monday, he instructed his staff to remove the discs, which came away easily with the application of a hot knife, and Dublin Dairies notched up a little victory in the sneaky Cold War.

In 1966, the frontline shifted when Dublin Dairies merged with Merville and Tel-el-Kebir to form Premier Dairies, with the new Premier Ice Creams taking on HB and Palm Grove.

1960S
TOP 5 SWEETS

1 SMITHS CRISPS

In 1963, Smiths relaunched in Ireland with its 'new' crisps priced threepence and an ad campaign featuring an image of the threepenny bit illustrated with a hare. Through the rest of the decade, Smiths would run competitions based on *Thunderbirds*, *The Man from U.N.C.L.E.* and other hit kids' TV shows.

2 THE ICEBERGER

Launched in 1968, the Iceberger seemed like a novel departure to a young generation, but in fact the ice cream sandwich was a concept going back to the start of the century.

3 TWIX

The two-fingered Twix was launched in the Summer of Love, 1967, when the Beatles, Stones and the flower-power generation were giving a different sort of two fingers to the establishment.

4 THE MAXI TWIST

Served in a plastic tub, this multicoloured swirl of ice cream mimicked the portions which had been served for some time to cinema audiences. Launched in 1968, the Maxi Twist was essentially the Mini Twist rebranded with a bigged-up name.

5 AZTEC BAR

Made of chocolate, nougatine and caramel, the Aztec first appeared in 1967 and stayed around for just eleven years. For the launch, lifesize Aztec warriors made of cardboard stood guard outside shops.

SWEET MEMORIES
BRIGID COUGHLAN, THE 1960s

I grew up in the 1960s era of the weekly wage, and Friday was payday for my dad. It was tradition for us five kids to give him our 'Friday order' each week for our comic and bar of chocolate. The excitement when my dad came home each week was intense.

It was Mandy *for me,* The Victor *for my brother and* Twinkle *for my little sister. The two youngest ones got flat picture books or Ladybirds until they were old enough to order a comic. It was a mortal sin to look at anyone's comic before they had read it through and we would all wait impatiently until each was finished and swap. My bar of choice was Fry's Chocolate Cream, though I remember going through a Roval phase (these were made by Urney's and were a bit like Rolos only oval). My brother and sister went for a variety of Cadbury's bars with Mint Crisp, Golden Crisp and Dairy Milk the favourites. There was always serious studying of any new varieties of sweets in our local shop for the weekly order. We tried Two & Twos for a while, which I think were made by Urney's but we always went back to the old favourites. When I think of it now, it must have been a nightmare for our dad, though I don't ever remember him getting the orders wrong. During Lent, we had to order fruit instead of sweets except for the nearest Friday to St Patrick's Day when we were allowed our chocolate order for the 'special day off'.*

An earlier memory was shopping with my mother midweek in Haugh's on the Crumlin Road when she would buy two of the small flat bars of Cadbury's and share them with us all. This was a huge treat.

Money was tight, as it was for everyone, but we always had a packet of biscuits after dinner each evening. Jacob's

Raspberry and Cream and Custard Creams at the beginning of the week with Marietta biscuits on Thursdays, for obvious reasons. Biscuits were always evenly distributed between the seven of us, so depending on how many were in the packet you could get anything from three (Marietta) to one-and-a-quarter (Raspberry and Creams). Fairness was everything in our house!

SWEET MEMORIES
ARTHUR MATHEWS, THE 1960s

Sweets! Curly Wurly (unforgettable name), fruit pastilles, wine gums, Brunches, choc ices. I loved Brunches (I'm delighted they're still around in the twenty-first century) but my main memory of ice cream is going into shops (especially a place down the road, Rafferty's – not even a proper shop, as it was only open during the summer) where the owner would 'create' a concoction (or 'concoct' a creation) for the customer by dividing up a rectangular HB block into slices, and placing wafers carefully at both ends. Biting into the wafer seemed to push out the ice cream from all sides, so the excess was usually licked off before the crispy, rectangular semi-casing could be properly tackled. (It also meant the item always had to be held sideways.)

Opal Fruits were exotic. Orange! Lemon! Lime! (I would have freaked out if I'd ever seen these television ads in colour). I think (the memory can play tricks) these were unavailable in Ireland until I was about sixteen. (Later, I believe, they were renamed Starbursts.) Juicy Fruits were an attractive, but not quite as exotic, Irish alternative.

Also – I think Milky Bars (advertised by bespectacled blond-child gunslinger The Milky Bar Kid – the most unthreatening cowboy ever) were also unavailable until my later teenage years. White chocolate! Wow.

At school, I remember loving King crisps. Some of the more adventurous boys (the type who may even have had girlfriends) mixed these in with peanuts (Manhattan?) to create an exotic mixture which I don't recall having a name — but surely should have.

My worst childhood sweet memory (literally a bitter-sweet memory) concerned a can of Apla, a Cadbury's Flake and a couple of spoonfuls of sugar.

Apla, by way of explanation, because I think the product doesn't exist any more, was an apple-based drink, probably similar to Cidona.

I remember, at the time, very much liking Cadbury's Flakes (still do) and sugar (still do a bit, but not as much). Apla was an unknown quantity to me, so I don't know why I went on an unsupervised Flake, Apla and sugar binge. I just remember being very sick afterwards. It still makes me queasy to think of it. (This probably happened around 1972.)

Yeeuuuchhhhhhhhhhh.

CHAPTER SIX

1970S
MADE IN ENGLAND

C ountless Irish children growing up in the 1960s shared a strange sense of being invisible to the wider world – the outside world for most Irish kids meant specifically our nearest neighbour, England.

Most of the best things seemed to come from England – the *Beano*, *Dandy*, *Sparky* and *Bunty*, the pop hits on the radio, *Match of the Day*, *Blue Peter*, *Top of the Pops*. Most of the best things, but generally not the sweets that were beamed into Irish living rooms every night in adverts that got brighter, catchier and more glamorous with the coming of colour television to both the BBC and ITV in 1969.

Spangles, Skybars, Swizzels Double dips, Texan bars, Minstrels, Revels and a host of other sweets flashed before our young eyes, but it was mostly a case of you can look but you cannot touch.

All that was changing rapidly by the start of the 1970s when a new trade pact with Britain led to a deluge of British sweets into Ireland that had the country's confectionery manufacturers up in arms. In 1970, Fine Gael in opposition asked the Fianna Fáil government if they were aware that the native sweet-making industry was being buried in the deluge, and what was being done about it. The minister confirmed that imports of British sweets had skyrocketed by a factor of six in four years,

SWEET MEMORIES

DAVID TWAMLEY, LEMON'S SWEETS SALES REP, 1970S

In Ulysses, his love letter to Dublin, James Joyce has his flawed hero Leopold Bloom drool over the Lemon's emporium which stood at the heart of Sackville Street. He wrote: 'Pineapple rock, lemon platt, butterscotch. A sugarsticky girl shovelling scoopfuls of creams for a christian brother. Some school treat. Bad for their tummies. Lozenge and comfit manufacturer to His Majesty the King. God. Save. Our. Sitting on his throne, sucking red jujubes white.'

At the start of the 1970s, David Twamley joined Lemon's in Drumcondra just when the company was already under threat from a tidal wave of foreign imports. Today, he still markets the Lemon's brand, but under the umbrella of the international Robert Roberts firm. He describes himself with some pride as 'the last man standing of old Lemon's'.

His earliest sweet memory was of how: 'My father used to live on sugared almonds. He'd have them in his pocket with his piped tobacco. He'd often hand me one and there'd be a smell of tobacco off it.

'There was a little shop called Norton's around the corner from us. It was run by a little man with a smiley face and a white coat. We used to collect jam jars. You'd bring in two jam jars and he'd give you a penny toffee. He'd take the jam jars out the back and we'd go out the back and take the jam jars and get another penny toffee. He was getting the same jam jars going around in circles.'

This is Saturday— I must get my—

Lemon's
PURE SWEETS

As a teenager, David was well aware of the Lemon's factory in nearby Drumcondra as a major, smelly, local landmark.

He says: 'When I was about sixteen, I got a summer job delivering milk with Premier Dairies in Finglas and one of our calls was the Lemon's factory. I can remember bringing milk up and having a cup of tea in the Lemon's canteen, and all the women in their white coats and their hairnets.

'A huge percentage of the workers there were women working at rows of machinery. The sweets were all poured into scales and weighed by hand before the bag machines took over. It was all very antiquated.

'It was a job for life. You went in from school and you stayed until you died. It was great crack. There was a great family atmosphere in the place. Generations of the same families went into the place. That's a bygone thing now in a lot of companies. People cared about each other and looked out for each other.'

Living some miles away, David doesn't remember the water changing colour from the dyes used, but he does remember the pungent odours which could waft surprisingly long distances. He says: 'I remember the smells. The smells were incredible. When they were making Arctic Mints or some of these things there was a whiff all over the place.'

Even as late as the start of the 1970s when he joined, practices took place which would never be tolerated today. He says: 'In the days before recycling if something went wrong and you were making a boiling of, say, mint, and you put too much mint in it, many's the boiling that went out the window and into the Tolka.

'They would do different runs of sweets on different tables. Every boiling was a hundredweight. They'd make a boiling of, say, mint. It would come out as a blob like hot plastic. With the souvenir mint it started as a big blob on the table and they'd put in the word Bray perhaps a foot thick and they'd build that into this blob, and the guys would stretch it out on these long tables until it was thirty or forty feet long and they'd leave it there to cool.

'It was twenty boxes of rock to the boiling and we, the merchandisers, would go around the country selling it. Lemon's had the rock business sewn up for the whole country.

'The owner of the company when I started was Frank Tate and he ran quality control himself. He'd go around the factory in a white coat and white hat and he'd walk around the tables and he'd pick up a cream toffee, put it in his mouth and suck it and chew it. That was quality control in those days.'

Quality was always the hallmark of Lemon's. Recalling his early years as a sales rep working mainly in the west of Ireland, he says: 'You had a lot of factories making kiddies' sweets, which wasn't really Lemon's business. They were making Flash Bars and other lines that kids were buying for twopence. Lemon's was always known as a quality product. They did things like the Big Five Bar which was like a Mars bar. They did Gems which were like Spangles which were twopence a packet.'

David came into the sweets trade at a time when there were still plenty of old-timers around to recount tales of less cut-throat times. He says: 'Some of the old guys at Lemon's told me that, during the Second World War when petrol was very scarce, they'd meet on a Monday morning – Clarnico, Richies and Rowntree Mackintosh. They'd travel to Cork in one car and plan their journey around the city for the day so that they wouldn't cross each other's paths. Then they'd meet up that evening, stay overnight and move on to the next town.'

At the start of the 1970s, some things hadn't changed much from the days of the Second World War, and even earlier. He says: 'When I started, Lemon's had a stand at the RDS Horse Show and the Spring Show every year. They had maybe five or six girls on it in uniform. I remember working on that stand and you'd be murdered all day with thousands of people buying sweets. That would have been the middle of the 1970s. They had a big carousel going around and round with sweets stuck on it.'

David Twamley was sill travelling around the country in the 1970s doing window displays of Lemon's sweets, which were old fashioned at the time but have come back with a vengeance. He fondly recalls: 'They used to have dummies. As merchandisers we put them in the windows. It was a piece of cardboard clipped into an actual box. There were sweets stuck all over the cardboard so it looked like the box was full. You'd leave them in the window until they'd go rotten and take them out and bin them. It was cheaper to use real sweets than anything else. Every year they'd have a confectioners' ball in the Shelbourne or the Gresham or some other hotel. It was a massive, very flashy event.'

But by the end of the 1970s, it had died as all the companies closed down or moved out. David recalls: 'The demand was far greater than the supply, but within a very few short years of joining the EEC in 1973, there were names coming into the country that you'd never heard of before like Ferrero Rocher, with massive organisations behind them *like Kraft and Nestlé, and the home producers were just crucified. It was very quickly becoming uneconomical to produce confectionery in Ireland. The wages here were off the wall and they were turning out stuff in huge quantities in Britain and they just saw Ireland as the equivalent of Greater Manchester.*

'The Irish manufacturers had very old equipment and antiquated systems and you could see at the start of the 1970s that they were going to go belly up very quickly.'

David reports that when the trade barriers went down, the country was 'blitzed' with cheaper, though maybe not better, sweets. He says: 'When I started, the Lemon's Season's Greetings line was a massive, massive Christmas seller. There just wasn't anything else out there to compete. I remember building displays in Dunnes of Henry Street and as you were taking the cellophane off you were handing them to people who were in a queue to get them.

'Within a few years it all went belly up.'

David Twamley recalls: 'The 1980s spelled the end for the Lemon's factory which had been a community centre in north Dublin for decades. There was 127 people there when the factory closed. They nearly all lived in the area, many in Millmount Place. There were houses all along Millmount Place and in the mornings you'd see them coming into the house and into the factory in their hairnets and then back home for lunch. All very local stuff. There was an incredible family atmosphere.'

but insisted that this was one of the prices we must pay for entry into Europe.

By the middle of the decade even vaster quantities of exotic British sweets, chocolates and toffees were flooding into the Republic, and this time it wasn't just the factory owners who were livid, but the sweetshop owners. Sweet sales fell off dramatically in the counties north of a line from Galway to Dublin, as tens of thousands of hard-pressed householders began buying cheap and in bulk from booming market towns straddling the border.

Consumers also took to buying their ice cream in bulk during the 1970s as a craze for home-freezing swept the land.

In 1953, there were thirteen ice cream manufacturers supplying the needs of Limerick alone. By 1973, that figure was down to four − and shrinking, although small local manufacturers still held on strongly in some areas. For instance, Leadmore Ice Cream based in the County Clare town of Kilrush still had a big hold on Limerick with its Super Softees, Twist Cups and Super Splits, while its three-ounce Super Choc was such a popular  favourite that HB started producing its own extra-size three-ounce choc ice especially for Limerick while selling its regular two-ounce choc ice everywhere else in the country.

But as protective tariffs were phased out, many independent Irish confectionery firms went to the wall or were taken over by the big international players. In 1973, for example, HB Ice Cream, which itself had earlier absorbed Urney Chocolates, was taken over by the global giant Unilever. Already an endangered species, the big old jars of loose bull's eyes, aniseed balls, clove rocks, torpedoes, kola cubes and cough drops went the way of the 78 disc and the trams.

One sign that Ireland was now part of the broader sweets market came when red M&Ms vanished from the packs on sale in the late 1970s, after Soviet boffins made a cancer link to Red Dye No. 2. Such was the force of the worldwide scare, that Mars pulled their red M&Ms even though the coloured buttons had never contained Red Dye No. 2 in the first place. It would be a full decade before the full spectrum was restored.

1970s Assortment

Decimalisation Day: When Two and Three Both Made One

Monday, 15 February 1971 was Decimalisation Day.

I will always look back on it as Disaster Day, when a little bit of my childhood was stolen by the grumpy old skinflint who owned a local sweetshop (not The Little Owl).

But more of that later.

Decimalisation was sold to the Irish public not just as a step on the path towards membership of the European Community, but as a very good thing in itself and, in many ways, it was.

It banished the most awkward and convoluted monetary system ever known to mankind. In the old way of doing things, a pound was made up 240 pennies subdivided into twenty shillings made up of half-crowns, bobs, tanners, ha'pennies and so on. The system wasn't called LSD for nothing.

The complexity of the coinage meant that, since time

immemorial, the whole thrust of learning sums at primary level was towards mastery of the twelve times table. For myself and every other kid at national school, these were grim times of rote learning by endless, mindless repetition that eleven elevens was 121 and twelve twelves was 144. In absolute contrast, decimalisation was a doddle.

It took about two days to master the new decimal tables, but we were given two years before D-Day to master it. Maths class went from being the second-most-hated, after Irish, to being the second-most-loved, after classes where the teacher phoned in sick and we were told to read quietly.

But while learning maths had suddenly become much easier for the nation's pupils, the practicalities of buying sweets would prove a nightmare. The staple of every child's pocket money was the sixpence coin stamped with a wolfhound and the Irish word 'reul'. This had an exact decimal equivalent of two and a half new pence. After that, however, things got complicated. One new penny was now to stand in for both two old pennies and three old pennies. Two new pence was both four old pence and five old pence. Four new pence replaced nine old pence and ten old pence. (You probably had to be there.)

The government assured a sceptical public that the nation's shopkeepers could be trusted to 'round up and round down' their prices, with the result that items going up would be balanced by those going down.

This was pie-in-the-sky piffle, as the opposition Labour TD Jim Tully pointed out to the Dáil three months before D-Day. Citing the magazine *Irish Decimal Monthly*, he said 'it gives a lot of information and many a laugh'. One issue, he said, featured a sketch of a shop window with a sign saying 'All Prices Rounded Down'. The shopkeeper had a halo above his head.

Tully remarked: 'If he reduces his prices, he will be entitled to a halo because he will be the only one in the country who will reduce prices. The minister is also entitled to a halo if he is so innocent as to think that there will be a reduction in prices. It is all right advising shopkeepers that they should not overcharge and that they should try to level off. That if they take a little extra from one customer they will give the article at a little less to the next customer. The minister knows that is not in accordance with human nature. It is more likely that 99 per cent of them will increase the price up to the next coin.'

As D-Day approached, a new industry grew up in preparing businesses, shoppers, school children and everyone else for the momentous changeover. New machines came on the market which could convert transactions from LSD to decimal and back again. 'Decimal Dawdlers' in business were warned they would 'pay the penalty'. In short, D-Day was presented as the Y2K event of its time – a ticking deadline likely to bring disaster to the unprepared.

For many sweetshop owners, D-Day was very much a case of taking two steps forward, one step back. The cash register was a relatively new feature on a lot of shop counters around the country, and now shopkeepers were being told that the ones they had were of no use anymore and they'd have to get them converted or buy new, decimal ones. The official advice to these retailers was that if they had to go back 'to the shoe box or cash drawer' for a few months, no harm would be done.

One consultancy service took out adverts counting down the number of working days to D-Day. The conductors on CIÉ's buses complained that they didn't understand the new fare prices, that neither would many of their customers, and the crews threatened that when the big day arrived, they'd refuse to handle the new coinage.

A woman with a vegetable stall on Dublin's Moore Street predicted that decimalisation would go the same way as decentralisation, quipping: 'It's like moving the civil service to the country. They said they would but no one really believes them.'

When 15 February 1971 finally arrived, it seemed that everyone in the land was in possession of at least ten ready reckoners. Most of these converting devices were strips of plastic or laminated cardboard like small school rulers, with the old LSD prices aligned with the new decimal ones. The more sophisticated were discs which could be manipulated to establish that a box of Liquorice Allsorts now priced $12\frac{1}{2}$ new pence would set you back two-and-six in old money.

There were delays in department stores and corner shops as customers and shopkeepers grappled with the strange coins. Unusually, one of the few areas which didn't suffer delays was the bus service. Bus crews who had pledged not to deal in the new money dropped their threat, and reported that passengers had a full grasp of the changed situation.

The country's main supermarket chains – H. Williams, Quinnsworth, Five Star, Superquinn and Liptons – reported an equally smooth changeover. Superquinn boss Feargal Quinn said that one elderly customer had refused to accept her change in the new money, but that the Decimal Courtesy kiosks he'd set up in each branch had been a big success. His checkout girls had all taken special courses and while the older ones, over the age of twenty-three, had been a little slow on the uptake, 'the seventeen year olds had no trouble'.

But by the time the momentous day was over, the worst fears of the country's youngest citizens had been realised. That morning's newspapers carried an advert by Cadbury which spoke of 'uneven conversions' and 'precise inclusions' and other grown-up things that wouldn't have been easily understood by the average school kid. It's meaning was simple enough, however – prices were going up.

And so back to my grumpy skinflint of a sweetshop owner. After school on D-Day, I found myself standing before his high walnut counter asking for my usual treat, but, this time, with the decimal coins in the palm of my hand that were so new they shone like gold.

I can't precisely recall what I asked for. It could have been a Trigger bar, or a Macaroon bar, or some candy-coated liquorice torpedoes. He set them down on the counter and told me the price.

And guess what?

Yep. He'd callously rounded all his prices upwards, and was wearing an ugly smirk rather than his customary sneer, rubbing in my devastation with relish.

Utterly betrayed and dismayed, I left swearing never to darken his door again. Which I probably didn't.

Two days later, it emerged that other confectionery manufacturers who had seemed to be charging the same in new money as in old had sneakily used the changeover to substitute smaller portions in lighter packages.

It was the day a generation of children lost their innocence.

Crates of Crunchies

On the first day of 1973, Ireland joined the European Economic Community. By the dying days of that torrid year, the country was in the grip of a global oil crisis that no one saw coming. In between, the food sector was thrown into a tumult which, amongst other things, had a dramatic effect on the nation's sweet-eating habits.

The candles lit in every household that Christmas had little to do with the festive, feel-good factor and everything to do with the daily power cuts that could last ten minutes or ten hours. Many workers were on a three-day week. Long queues snaked around kerbs for rationed petrol. Late-night television was deemed an extravagance so RTÉ scrapped a lump of its Christmas schedule in the hope of sending everyone to bed early.

The twin bright spots for me and the rest of Ireland's children that Christmas were that the power cuts provided the perfect excuse for doing no homework, and the school holidays were extended by a week to save the state precious heating fuel.

From the start of the 1970s, price-conscious house-holders had been investing in big home freezers which had enabled them to save on their weekly shopping bill by buying burgers, chicken, fish, vegetables and other food stuffs in bulk. The Corless home freezer was humped into the garage on the sound principles that it was far too big for the kitchen and it made a sound like a lawnmower. I vividly recall returning from fishing trips off Skerries on my Uncle Fergie's small boat, weighed down with perhaps 200 mackerel on a very good day. I'd go up and down the road with buckets of mackerel asking the neighbours if they'd take some. The rest went into the big freezer. But for the next few tea-times, the pungent smell of pan-fried mackerel would settle over the entire road.

As the fuel crisis took hold and food and fuel prices soared, the home freezer seemed to make even better sense. In late 1973, *The Irish Times* recommended that canny householders should buy gallon tubs of ice cream, available direct from HB, mix in fruit and eat at their leisure.

The whole mixing business seemed like a lot of work, so we just bought the tubs of ice cream.

Runaway inflation, short-time factory working and a convoluted system of new European food subsidies meant that, by the middle of 1974, the newspapers were full of stories that milk and sugar rationing was on the way. By the start of 1975, a shortage of drinking milk had become a reality because Brussels was paying Irish farmers top dollar to divert their milk into chocolate, yoghurt and other sidelines.

Meanwhile, the same European subsidies led to a crazy situation where butter manufactured in the Republic was on sale in Northern Ireland at a far lower price than in the Republic. Shoppers from Dublin, Galway, Drogheda, the midlands, the border counties and farther afield began making a weekly trek northwards.

The tiny townland of Jonesboro straddling the border between south Armagh and Louth became a Mecca for southerners in search of a bargain, the Corless family included.

For a while, the trip to Jonesboro replaced the family Sunday drive to Dollymount Strand or up the Dublin Mountains. The traffic would thicken a couple of miles out, to the point that my dad would start to park perhaps a mile out of the hamlet and we'd all walk the last stretch. That walk took us along narrow roadways choked with cars and private coaches that had to keep moving forward at a snail's pace because there was no room to reverse. It was like a premonition of what it would be like going to a rock concert when rock concerts eventually came to Ireland.

While some punters came for the two-stone boxes of butter, others stayed to browse the new-fangled colour televisions which, at £200, cost half the price of those you could get in the South. Radios and record players blared from stalls and shop fronts. Under EEC rules, it was illegal to import goods over the value of £52 into the Republic, but the ordinary rule of law didn't extend to the Republican stronghold of south Armagh and thousands took their chances with a new television in the car boot.

Amusingly, the standard line from the figures running the Jonesboro market was that they were in the charitable business of raising money to repair the local parish church. After five minutes touring the honky-tonk joint, it was blindingly obvious that enough profit was being generated to build a new Vatican City off the plans.

No day trip was complete without a crate of Crunchies or Kit-Kats, but the greatest prize of all was a month's supply of Spangles or the many other English sweets that we saw on British television programmes but never in the Irish shops.

The Jonesboro phenomenon proved, even to the most sweet-addicted child, that you really can have too much of a good thing. When officialdom finally managed to lob a spanner in the works, many children gave a small sigh of relief that never again would they watch their dad produce another factory carton of Wagon Wheels from the boot of his grimy Cortina.

Mister Tayto and The Man From U.N.C.L.E.

The cutting-edge gimmick of crisp makers in the 1960s and 1970s was the TV tie-in where you could save up some random number of crisp packets and send them away for a fabulous prize.

Smiths Crisps were the masters of this marketing ploy and I can remember their promotions for *Thunderbirds*, *Joe 90* (I think) and *The Man from U.N.C.L.E.*

The back of Smiths' Thunderbirds packs featured illustrations of the four futuristic International Rescue

SWEET MEMORIES
JOSEPH O'CONNOR, THE 1970s

Helen McBride
Angel of the sweetshop.
Dispenser of joys.
Seventeen that summer.
In the eyes of us boys
She was luscious as a wine gum.
Hands on her hips.
Sweet-cigarette
Between her cherry bomb lips.

Love Hearts on the counter.
Chocolate on the shelf.
She asked me what I wanted
And I nearly gulped, 'Yourself.'
But at fifteen, I couldn't
For my tongue got tied.
So I lied and said 'a Twix Bar'
And ate it outside.

Postcards in the window
Of donkeys and bogs.
A seaside town in summertime.
Lost, trotting dogs.
Glancing through the glass
At the girl of my dreams
And she laughing with a garda,
Sharing lemon ice creams.

Wished I was her fellah.
Wished I was her prince.
Wished I could be sharing
Fox's Glacier Mints
With the sweetest girl in Galway
And we kissing on the beach
Where her lips would taste of liquorice
And apple-drops and peach.

Gob-stopping beauty,
Curly-Wurly locks.
Cute among the Kit-Kats
And the souvenir rocks.
'I Visited Salthill' was the message inside.
But written on my heart was 'Helen McBride'.

Irish Colleen with Donkey and Turf Baskets

crafts. Each of these 'clip-together scale models' was on offer to anyone who sent away the requisite number of Smiths packets plus a postal order for one shilling and threepence.

I had no interest in the crude puppets of *Thunderbirds* who each combined wooden acting with a bad case of delirium tremens, but *The Man from U.N.C.L.E.* had everything a young boy could look forward to when he was old enough to leave school and get his first job as a glamorous, gun-toting, globe-trotting secret agent.

So I collected the required number of crisp packets, got my parents to fetch me a postal order, and sent away to an address in England, and waited.

I went to bed that night deliriously happy that in no time I'd have my U.N.C.L.E. badge in the name of Illya Kuryakin (Napoleon Solo was too smug and all-American), an ID card signed by U.N.C.L.E. boss Alexander Waverly and, best of all, a circular embossed cardboard decoder which could be used to unscramble the accompanying letter from Smiths warning of the threat to the Free World posed by the evil plotters of THRUSH whose aim was 'the subjugation of humanity'.

And I waited. And waited.

As the weeks turned to months, I became more and more inconsolable, to the point where my parents, driven to distraction by me, wrote a stern letter to Smiths in England demanding they send my spy kit.

And then, one magical day, it finally arrived and I became Illya Kuryakin, flashing my badge and ID card to jealous classmates in the schoolyard and generally decoding everything from the lead story in The Irish Times to the ingredients on the back of the Cornflakes box.

I kept that circular cardboard decoder well into my teens, although I didn't use it quite as much by then.

The Cheese & Onion Crisp – Ireland's Gift to the World

In 1972, Ireland's potato crisp wars, which had been simmering for a decade, came to the boil when Tayto took Perri to court and charged them with impersonation. Tayto were the undisputed heavyweight champions of the native crisp market, accounting for seven out of every ten packs sold. Perri were the upstart newcomers, accused of designing their Mr Perri mascot to closely resemble the established Mr Tayto.

The judge found in favour of Tayto and granted an injunction forbidding Perri from selling their crisps in lookalike packs.

Four decades on, the Irish are munching through an average three packets of crisps each week, most of them Tayto, and the odd-shaped Yellowman with the red hat has made the leap from decorating a crisps packet to becoming a fully fledged Irish cultural icon. The 2009 number one Christmas bestseller was Mr Tayto's spoof autobiography, which outsold all-comers including *The Guinness Book of Records*.

Meanwhile, Tayto Park near Ashbourne in County Meath which opened in 2010 has become an unlikely tourist attraction, with thousands of families pouring through the turnstiles on summer days for the carnival turns and the menagerie of exotic animals.

In the normal scheme of things, an adventure park commemorating potato crisps might seem a bit, well, over the top. But Tayto is no ordinary potato crisp. In fact, the Tayto potato crisp is one of Ireland's great gifts to the world in the past century.

The mastermind behind Tayto was Joe 'Spud' Murphy, a Dubliner who single-handedly changed the face of confectionery the world over. At the age of twenty during the Second World War, Murphy spotted that there was no Ribena available in Ireland. He somehow got his hands on a supply and took his first step to becoming one of Ireland's richest men.

The first potato chips sold commercially appeared in the United States around 1908. They came in boxes and tins and quickly went stale. The first crisp packets, also from the US, were made of wax paper sheets stapled into the shape of a bag. Crisps as we know them were invented around 1920 by Smiths Crisps of London. They came in one flavour – potato.

Founder Frank Smith tried to counter the blandness by packaging a paper twist of salt with his slivers of potato in the bag. This was a taste sensation in its day and the salt-your-own crisps were a big hit in London and quickly spread to Ireland and beyond.

Joe Murphy was an avid muncher of crisps but complained that they were bland and boring. Shaking on a sprinkle of salt was okay, so far as it went, but there had to be a better way. Murphy's solution was to create the world's first flavoured potato crisp, Tayto Cheese & Onion. He started production in Dublin with one van and eight employees, persuading the Findlater chain of upmarket stores to stock his new crisps.

Tayto Cheese & Onion crisps were an overnight sensation, not just in Ireland but around the world. Senior executives from crisp companies abroad flocked to Murphy's door to buy a piece of the action.

Murphy poured his new-found wealth back into marketing the company. Tayto's sponsored radio programmes like *Leisure Time* ('Take it easy with Tayto') and *Cruising With Tayto* became staples of the schedules.

Tayto neon signs became part of the urban landscape. School rulers stamped with the Tayto logo circulated in classrooms.

And now a theme park. A monument too far?

Hardly. The Cheese & Onion crisp – part of who we are.

Catch Them While You Can

By 1970, the Urney Chocolates factory in Tallaght, Dublin, was being run out of business by the flood of British imports which followed the dropping of import tariffs. For decades, Urney's had prospered behind the protective tax wall which kept foreign competition out of the Irish market. The Tallaght firm often turned a profit by knocking out Irish ringers for British brands, producing the Roval to rival Rowntree's Rolos while Urney's Beanos bore more than a passing resemblance to Rowntree's Smarties.

Sometimes, Urney's plucked an idea from the air that they could proudly call their own, and their extra wide Two & Two bar was a multicoloured, multilayered delight combining dessert and milk chocolate, cream fudge and vanilla fondant. In 1975, now under the HB banner, the Tallaght team came up with another innovative winner, the Catch Bar. The Catch Bar quickly became a bestseller on the back of a television ad campaign with a catchy jingle that built on the hook: 'Catch it if you can, first it's crispy/Catch it if you can, then it's creamy.' And so on.

Cadbury's negotiated the 1970s in better shape than Urney's, although the tariff changes meant the company, which had employed 3,000 people a decade earlier, increasingly became an importer of favourite Cadbury's lines from Britain.

The market leader, Dairy Milk, was still produced in Ireland, as was Snack which became Cadbury's best-selling home-made treat by the end of the decade. Other local lines, such as the Tonga and Swiss Bars, came and went in the blink of an eye.

Another homespun television advert of 1975 gave a shot in the arm to another singular Irish product, Silvermints, which had been around since the 1920s. The colourful comic strip advert featured cool clean hero Steve Silvermint wiping the floor with some ugly sweets ganging up on a defenceless woman and her child. Sales of Silvermints soared.

While HB Chocolates struggled through the 1970s, its ice cream-making wing thrived by hitching their ice pops to the ever-changing fads and gimmickry of pop culture. A Super Split wrapper might bring you a prize, while the Fiddlestix range were ice lollies on plastic sticks moulded to fit together like pieces of the building toy Meccano.

The Fizzy Fred ('Puts a tingle on your tongue'), Flavour Raver ('Four super flavours in one super pop') and Tip Top ('You'll love the jelly') were multicoloured multilayered creations that paved the way for two of the decade's true blockbusters, the Wibbly Wobbly Wonder and the Loop The Loop.

Between 1973 and 1977, HB alone launched twenty-five new ices onto a crowded marketplace, including the Pet Pop (featuring a pooch), Twicer (kangaroo), Dracula (fanged ghoul), Ko Ko Mo (palm tree), Little Angel, Little Devil and Kung Fu. The latter featured a Bruce Lee figure on the wrapper and had a cool black belt

running through the lolly itself. In the cut-throat world of youth fads, the sales curve of many ice pops resembled that of The Bay City Rollers, except shorter. The Toffee Tuffy, for instance, arrived with a thundering bang in

SWEET MEMORIES
TONY CONSIDINE, THE 1970s

I used to love getting the packs of Topps trading cards with footballers or scenes from films like Star Wars *that came with a stick of pink chewing gum. You could get the smell of the gum as soon as you opened the packet, the smell of it was nearly nicer than the taste of it!*

See-Threepio and Luke

Our local shop in Malahide was Stan's and my favourite sweets were Trigger bars and Gold Rush bubble gum. It was the bag the gum came in as much as anything that made it for me. It was a cut above the usual packaging with a drawstring on it – very exciting for a six or seven year old!

I wasn't impressed when they changed the name of Trigger bars to Chomp. I guess it came with the whole cowboy and

1975 with sales in excess of 15 million. A year later, the teenybop generation had moved on, and the Toffee Tuffy languished unloved and unwanted in freezers across the nation.

Indian thing going a bit out of fashion. The early- to mid-1970s were probably the last hurrah for that.

I also remember getting Bazooka Joe chewing gum and there being a short comic strip inside the wrapper. If you collected enough wrappers you could send away for different things. I got my first camera through Bazooka Joe. It only took black and white pictures. Colour film wouldn't work in it!

Other memories include being allowed two sweets from a Clery's bag on a weekly visit to my gran's, or three if you were lucky, generally bon bons, iced caramels or Murray Mints. The odd time there'd be a Murray's Spearmint which I loved. Though I always felt like hitting the jackpot, I never would have dared suggest that she bought them more often!

And, of course, there was hoarding your sweets during Lent but being allowed have a nibble on Paddy's Day. How many kids these days go through Lent without eating sweets? I think people were a lot more strict about it in our day.

1970S
TOP 5 SWEETS

1 CURLY WURLY
Described as resembling 'two flattened, intertwined serpentine strings' of chocolate-coated caramel, the Curly Wurly became arguably the signature bar of the 1970s. The adverts featuring comic Terry Scott clad as a schoolboy were as popular in Ireland as in Britain.

2 WIBBLY WOBBLY WONDER
Launched in 1974, this was a multi-layered ice pop with the top half coated in crunchy ice cream. Something of a sensation in the 1970s, it melted from view in the 1990s and was withdrawn, though it made a comeback 2006.

3 TWIRL
An Irish original, the Twirl is essentially a Flake in a chocolate casing. The first Twirls were singular, but following their rebranding as a twin bar in the 1980s, they have conquered the globe.

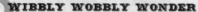

4 CATCH BAR
Born and bred in the Dublin suburb of Tallaght, the Catch Bar was created in 1976 in the HB Chocolate factory (formerly Urney's). It shot to the top of Ireland's bestseller list on the back of an infuriatingly catchy television ad ('Catch it if you can, first it's crispy . . .').

5 CADBURY FLAKE
Around since 1920, Flake had its heyday in the 1970s on the back of a racy television ad campaign featuring a young woman nibbling suggestively, accompanied by the ditty 'only the crumbliest, flakiest chocolate, tastes like chocolate never tasted before'.

SWEET MEMORIES
MICK FLANAGAN, THE 1970s

Growing up in the 1970s, sweets were a rarity in our house. The weekly grocery shop was conducted by modest means, and one thing was for sure: it never included sweets, fizzy drinks or crisps. And because we lived far away from our grandparents, aunts and uncles, my siblings and I hardly ever got random treats.

However, every Sunday, on the way home from mass, we would stop at a shop called Pick 'n' Choose, from which my mother would emerge with my father's Sunday newspaper and a packet of Cadbury's Chocolate Eclairs – not a bag, but a roll.

My four brothers, my sister and I would be squeezed into the back of our Ford Escort, slavering like children in a Dickensian workhouse as my mother opened the roll and doled out the sweets – two each and an odd one over, which she gave to a different one of us each week.

The treasured, toffee-chocolatey taste of those Eclairs still fills my mouth at the memory of it. For me, it was like being given a fleeting, tantalising shot of some deliriously exciting drug. I would be literally gagging for another fix.

As my mother held the final Eclair aloft, all of us would be bouncing up and down on the back seat shouting, 'Me! Me! Me!', even if we knew it was not our turn. When the final sweet was given out, we'd sit back down and forget it, not resentful or jealous of this week's favoured sibling, but already thinking about next Sunday and watching our mother emerge from Pick 'n' Choose, the Sunday Independent *under her arm and sweets in her pocket for all of us. There was no better feeling.*

CHAPTER SEVEN

1980S
GREED IS GOOD,
SIZE IS IMPORTANT,
IRISH IS OUT

Green, lime-flavoured and frog-shaped, the Fat Frog ice lolly was one of the sweet sensations of the 1980s. It was not to be confused with the Funny Foot, which was ice cream shaped like a foot with a chocolate-covered big toe. Another big seller was the lime-tinged strawberry sorbet launched in 1982 as the Tongue Twister, subsequently becoming the Tangle Twister before slimming down to just the Twister.

And don't forget the Nogger from 1982, a solid nugget of chocolate delight that was perfected by an additional casing of light and crunchy chocolate. Swiftly rebranded as The Feast, it remains a modern classic.

Launched in 1977, The Little Devil was a smash hit. But in terms of sheer ambition there was nothing to touch that company's 1983 creation, The Wicked Witch, which was touted as Ireland's first 3-D ice lolly. Sadly, this Wicked Witch went the way of the one in *The Wizard of Oz*.

Chocolate favourites spawned in the 1980s include the Moro Bar and the double-barrelled Twirl.

What's most significant about these 1980s treats was

that they were 100 per cent Irish in conception and manufacture. That made them rare indeed.

In 1983, the Lemon's Sweet Factory on the Drumcondra Road in Dublin shut its gates for the last time. Over the decades, it had become a landmark and a key local employer with a workforce of hundreds.

But that world was going, going . . .

Three years later, in 1986, future Taoiseach Albert Reynolds, then in opposition, accused the government of doing nothing to save the ailing confectionery industry. He said that if the sector closed, the farmers would have 30 million gallons of unsold milk lapping around their wellies, and the homespun sugarbeet industry would be ruined.

But it was all bluster because the horse had already bolted. Ireland's independence as a sweets-producing nation was buried under a landslide of cheap imported confectionery and corporate takeovers.

But while specialised sweetshops and independent Irish manufacturers had been wiped out by the 1980s, one newcomer showed that small could be beautiful and marked the way forward for today's retro sweetshop revival.

Actually, Butlers Chocolates was hardly a newcomer. The company was founded in Dublin in 1932. But, in 1984, the company rebranded, and launched Butlers Irish Chocolates as an upmarket luxury treat. The Celtic Tiger was still a decade away but the yuppie revolution was going full steam ahead in neighbouring Britain and the mood was infectious.

At precisely the same time, Ballygowan launched its bottled mineral water. People scoffed at the plainly barmy notion of paying for something that fell freely from the skies, but both Ballygowan and Butlers Irish Chocolates tapped into deep-seated aspiration.

In 1989, Butlers opened their first chocolate shop on Dublin's Grafton Street and soon they were all over Ireland, and moving into Britain. As such, Butlers provided the link between the specialist sweetshops of old and the retro sweetshops of today, entering the world of the 1980s as the plucky little individual taking on the might of the corporate giants.

Size was everything in the 1980s. In the movies, it was Arnie Schwarzenegger and Sylvester Stallone. In fashion, it was shoulder pads and big hair. And in keeping with the times, chocolate bars bulked up to Arnie proportions, while the latest hot items on the supermarket shelves were 'treat-size' bites that could only be bought by the sackful.

The Yorkie Bar was the trendsetter. Conceived as a chunkier rival to Cadbury's traditional Dairy Milk, it arrived in Ireland in 1979 having already driven Britain wild with its all-singing, all-motoring commercial featuring a square-jawed trucker. Cadbury's Ireland immediately responded by bringing out new beefed-up versions of Dairy Milk and other top lines, and promoting them with equally manly commercials featuring lumberjacks. Meanwhile the Mars bar, Marathon and Twix all upsized in order to size up to the competition.

Like everything else in the trade, marketing departments got more muscle-bound as the decade rolled on.

In 1979, the capital's tardy double-decker buses came in one colour – a sickly yellowish green. But that year some marketing bright spark had the clever idea of renting the entire surface of a bus as advertising space. And so, Dubliners were treated to the weird and wonderful sight of a CIÉ No. 19 spluttering down O'Connell Street in several shocking shades of blue, decorated with a landscape painting of a waterfall and bearing the legend 'I Like Spike'.

Launched by Cantrell & Cochrane that year, Spike was a wishy-washy fizzy concoction which was withdrawn after three years to be replaced by the equally dull Club 90.

In the summer of 1981, when buses took to the capital's streets in bright red livery and featuring a gondolier singing the slogan 'Just one Cornetto', the painted bus was still pretty much the last word in marketing innovation. By the end of the decade, it had become a quaint jalopy chugging along in the slow lane.

As the 1980s progressed, the hard-sell of sweets became at once more subtle and more blatant. Events like Mother's Day and Father's Day, which had never been given much pass by Irish consumers, were transformed by the marketers into major highpoints on the annual sales graphs. Over the course of the decade, Hallowe'en was successfully targeted by the marketing departments to the point that it shot from being just another so-so sales occasion to its current position as the third biggest annual bonanza for the Irish confectionery business after Easter and Christmas.

SWEET MEMORIES
JOHN MCMAHON, THE 1980s

Miggsy came running into school one morning, his mouth foaming with news. We watched with scepticism as he stood in front of us, hyperventilating Miggsy had a reputation for holding the truth in one hand, pinching it between the thumb and index finger of the other hand and stretching it until it became a thin string so frail that even the briefest of farts would blow it apart.

'Clock-Clock Bubbagub!' he panted. His glasses weren't just fogged; it looked like it was actually raining back there.

'What's that, Miggsy?'

He calmed down after a time. 'They have it in America. My dad saw it.'

'They have what, yeh spedge?'

'Chocolate bubblegum.'

We stood there blinking, letting the news work its way into our eleven-year-old synapses. Chocolate . . . bubblegum ... What? What?

What Wonka-esque alchemy was this? Two titans of taste — hitherto incommensurable and arguably locked in an antagonism greater than that of history itself — now somehow yoked together in a single, chewable lump? The ill-matched mother and father of all our candied memories now finally united in some idyllic confectionery matrimony? Like bubblegum itself, it was far too much to digest. How could it be true? It couldn't. We duly dismissed and dispatched the rumour-monger.

'Fuck up, Miggsy.'

But there was such a thing as chocolate bubblegum. I tasted it years later. It felt like bubblegum but didn't taste like chocolate. It tasted like chocolate flavouring — a mere representation of chocolate, a shadow of chocolate projected on a sweetshop wall, or how chocolate might be described to someone who's never tasted chocolate.

I wonder if Miggsy's still alive.

1980S
TOP 5 SWEETS

1 FAT FROG

Launched in 1981, the Fat Frog ice pop became a huge hit on the back of an advertising jingle which went: 'My name's Fat Frog. I live in a swamp and I play my guitar like a Fat Frog. He's got a big fat tummy like no other water ice, lots of fruity flavour from his toes to his eyes.' And so on . . .

2 WHAM BAR

A thin strip of chewy toffee with coloured crumbs of sherbet inside, the Wham Bar was launched in the early 1980s. It was probably sheer coincidence that an act called Wham! (with an exclamation mark) were the biggest pop group on the planet.

3 PUSH POPS

These were lollipops encased in pump-action plastic containers. The idea was to push the lolly bit by bit out of its shell. They came in varieties including Triple Power and Push Pump Spray and the slogan was: 'Push a Push Pop, push it for flavour, push a Push Pop, save some for later!

4 LEMONADE SPARKLE ICE POPS

They came in orange and white and were made with real fruit juices and had a lemony taste. Its mixture of sweetness and tanginess made it the perfect thirst quencher. They cost ten pence and they sparkled on the taste buds like lemonade.

5 DOUBLE DIPS

A reminder of a time when Double Dip didn't have anything to do with recession, these were a 1980s repackaging of the endlessly popular sherbet dip. They consisted of a twin pack of fizzy powder (cola, cherry, orange, etc.) and a swizzlestick for dipping and licking.

1980s Assortment

The War on Sweets

When Ireland's legislators returned from their lengthy Christmas holidays to face into the challenges of 1980, opposition-party Fine Gael set out their stall by declaring war on sweets. Deputy Michael Keating asked Minister for Health Michael Woods if he would take action to ban the sale of confectionery in the nation's school tuck shops. Sweets, he argued, were very bad for the health of children.

The minister said that the principal threat of sweet eating to children's health was that it caused dental decay. He added that 'consumption of sweets is of course a matter of personal choice' and that he favoured gentle persuasion rather than a ban.

The war on sweets had started in earnest eight years earlier with the publication of a book called *Pure, White and Deadly*. Penned by a pioneering professor of nutrition, John Yudkin, it opened with a statement in Chapter One that 'sugar is really dangerous'. Warming to his theme throughout, he closed with a chapter entitled 'Why Sugar Should Be Banned'.

Fine Gael's new-found interest in banning sugar came just months after a sensational murder case in the United States in which one San Francisco politician shot dead another in a dispute over who got to occupy the mayor's office. Dan White didn't deny the killing of Mayor George Moscone and another official, but his legal eagles put up what immediately became infamous as 'the Twinkie Defense'.

The defence argument was essentially that White had switched from a healthy diet to one based on fizzy drinks and candy bars, such as Twinkies, and the switch had turned this champion of law and order into a deranged killer.

The jury brought in a verdict of manslaughter instead of murder and he got off with five years in prison.

While the government insisted that it had no interest in preventing pupils from paying for sweets in their schools, the state had just begun depriving hospital patients of their free sweets and biscuits that had been a traditional feature of the hospital menu.

Asked about this, the Minister for Health read out 'the current diet' served to patients. Strikingly, at this remove, there was no choice of menu. Lunch consisted of 'soup, bacon, cabbage, potatoes, white sauce' while tea was 'fried bacon and potatoes'. No meat was served on Fridays 'when there is fish for lunch and beans on toast for tea'.

Pressed on the matter of why patients were being deprived of their sweets, the minister replied that these were 'not necessary in the current diet of patients'.

Having briefly taken up the cause of hospitalised sweet lovers, Fine Gael switched back to the attack in 1982, tackling the government on the sale of 'dangerous sweets'. Oversized gobstoppers known as 'gullies' or 'golf balls' had recently caused the deaths of two children and the party wanted them banned. The minister said he'd had a word with the trade about it and 'asked the Health Education Bureau to take account of this kind of danger in relation to their programme for accident prevention'.

And that was the last the Dáil heard on the subject.

SWEET MEMORIES
JOANNA SMYTH, THE 1980S AND 1990S

Mum taped a list of forbidden E numbers to our fridge and every time my brother and I bought a packet of sweets, we would religiously study the list. I remember planning a trip to our local shop specifically to inform them that there was a 'forbidden' E number listed in the ingredients for Black Jack sweets, and they shouldn't sell them anymore. I was nine years old and very self-righteous. Thankfully, my dad talked me out of it.

Things we weren't really allowed to have but occasionally berated Mum into buying for us included Stinger bars, Refreshers, Fruit Salad sweets, Apple Jacks, Black Jacks, Push Pops, and those lollipops that you would wear as a ring on your finger. Hubba Bubba chewing gum was also really popular. Again, Mum wasn't wild about us having it – mostly because we always managed to swallow it.

I remember Push Pops very well – the ad had a very catchy jingle and the tag line was 'Don't push me, push a Push Pop!' According to the ad, this sweet had the handy added bonus of solving the problem of bullying in schools. Push Pops were the sort of thing you would beg your mother for, but regret if she relented – you had to push your finger up into the tube to get the lolly out, and this was really unpleasantly sticky.

Kinder Eggs were also massively popular when I was young. They did a series of collectible toys (Teeny Terrapins was one of them) and me, my siblings and my friends were endlessly striving to acquire the entire set of each. You were always really devastated when you cracked open the Kinder Egg to find a figurine you already had. Our collection used to sit on top of the television.

Mr. Freeze ice pops were massive in the 1980s and people seemed to become re-obsessed with them later in secondary school, running across the road from school to the shop even during winter's coldest months to snap one up.

I loved chocolate. One summer, I set about a quest to try all the Cadbury bars – the only one I didn't enjoy was the Rum and Raisin (which I think has been discontinued, thankfully). I don't remember Snickers being called Marathons, but I do remember when they changed the name of Opal Fruits to Starburst – I don't think I have ever managed to call them Starburst. I also think I tried all of the Chewits flavours too – I even had a Chewits pencil case (blackcurrant flavour, if you're wondering).

After mass on Sundays, we would stop at our local shop on the way home to get sweets. I remember my mum usually wanted Fry's Chocolate Cream, which I also occasionally got (on days when I wanted to feel grown-up). During the summer, we would go for drives to Spiddal on Sundays and get ice cream (usually 99s) on the way home.

I remember once my grand-uncle came for a visit from Scotland, and brought us a massive box of Caramac bars. I think they were supposed to be caramel-flavoured chocolate – it was sort of a yellowy-cream colour. Anyway myself and my siblings were delighted . . . initially. After a few days, I never wanted to see another Caramac bar again. The number of bars contained in the box was endless. We used to actually hand them out to anybody who called to our house in an effort to get rid of them. Even when we succeeded, one of the cupboards in our kitchen still smelled like Caramac for weeks. Even thinking about them now makes me a little queasy!

Another range of sweets that me and my siblings were fascinated by were Nerds and Dweebs – I don't really remember what they tasted like. I think they were sour luminous-coloured chewy sweets that looked like little pebbles but had a chewing-gum-like consistency inside. I think mostly it was the name of the sweets that attracted us – we were huge fans of the Teenage Mutant Hero Turtles and this was the sort of vocabulary they used to insult each other.

Which leads me to . . . the Teenage Mutant Hero Turtles ice lollies which we loved, especially my brother. There were also Super Mario ice creams. Both characters were massively popular when I was young – cartoons, merchandise, video games so these had particular appeal to my age group.

Freedom Fighters to Facebook:
Kavanagh's Sweetshop

Kavanagh's sweetshop on Dublin's Aungier Street provides an unbroken line of continuity between the starting point of this book and the present day.

It opened its doors in 1925. The then plotter and future Taoiseach Seán Lemass would hold conspiratorial meetings in the smoke-filled tea room at the back.

The young Lemass had a special fondness for Orange Caramels.

In the late 1970s, a chimney sweep was at work there unblocking the soot and grime of decades. Ten-year-old Eddie Kavanagh was serving in the shop, as he had since the age of six.

He recalls: 'We heard this massive yell and this tumbling noise and it was the sweep coming flying down the chimney breast out into the shop. And lo and behold, lots of old army outfits and rifles and all the gear from that era came flying down with him. They'd been hidden up the chimney for decades. They're now on display in the National Museum.'

He says, 'The shop was opened by my grandfather Joeseph Kavanagh and his wife Theresa, who'd have come to Dublin in the 1910s. The first of four shops they opened was in Aungier Street and Theresa was the driving force. She went in to put the bid on the shop to buy it, and in those days it wasn't the done thing for the woman to be in that role.

'They opened in 1925 and in those days it was an old-style grocery shop with a tea room at the back. A lot of the women weren't allowed into pubs so they went to tea rooms to socialise. They did a lot of sandwiches, a bit of hot food, tea, coffee.'

Eddie followed his father into the family business, but others were forced onto the emigration trail. 'My uncle Edmund is quite prominent in America where he's known as what is a 'gold chaser' in the jewellery business. He'd have made a lot of jewellery for Frank Sinatra and his wife and he's made a chain that Mike Tyson wears.'

His father took over the store in the mid-1970s when the tea room had vanished and Kavanagh's main trade was weighing out sweets onto scales to be sold loose from the jar.

'I've got seven sisters and three brothers. We didn't have any staff. As soon as you were six years of age and you could reach that jar of sweets – because they were all kept on shelves above head height – you worked. We all lived above the shop and would have gone to school locally, so we'd all have worked in the shop every day after school.

'It was a business and it was a family business, but it was also a way of life. You met your friends in the shop. I remember people having singalongs in the shop.'

By 1978, at the age of ten, Eddie had a sense that his family sweetshop which still sold loose sweets from the jar was no longer the norm. 'When you were out and about, you realised that not every shop was like this. In my father's day, there could have been 250 or 300 different varieties of sweets. All Irish made. There were also some lines that came in from England.'

What happened next was an experience shared by both sweetshops and sweet manufacturers throughout the country.

'The big brands from abroad saw some lines and they wanted them. They might have only wanted 10 per cent of the products by a certain company, but they bought over these companies and they delisted a lot just to get their hands on that 10 per cent.'

He lists with a schoolboy's zest some of the sweets that suddenly became hard to find when the big boys from abroad moved in. 'Cough tablets, bull's eyes, clove rock, acid drops, pineapple chunks, kola cubes, dollie mixtures, aniseed balls, liquorice torpedoes.'

The demand for the old, loose sweets never died out, even at the height of the cash-rich, time-poor boom. He says: 'There was a great demand for the old loose sweets. People were coming from far and near. There was criticism from people when we changed the old look of the shop, but the fact was that a lot of the old wooden cabinets were falling apart. They had woodworm and all these problems and you couldn't keep them intact. So we had to go a more modern route, but we kept on all the sweets.'

Nostalgia, even at the height of the all-mod-cons Celtic Tiger, remained a potent force. According to Eddie: 'The sales of the sweets remained very good, and we have a lot of customers living abroad who will send an email and we'll put a package together. There's one customer who comes over from Los Angeles for Oatfield's chocolate orange sweets. That's the one she loves. She'll get five or six big jars of them packaged up and she ships them back.'

Eddie sees a bright future for the family sweetshop that opened in 1925. 'When credit is available, I'd like to turn the shop back into the old style traditional sweetshop. We have a Facebook site for the shop which is a good indicator of the interest we're getting in retro sweets.'

According to Kavanagh, retro sweets may have gone underground for a period, but they never really went away. The rise and rise of the retro sweetshops which are popping up all over the country comes to him as no surprise.

'If you look at the situation in general, it's a case that everybody is going back to the old values. Even the signage in windows is not as hi-tech or flash as it used to be. A lot of it is going back to only two colours. I notice that Oatfield have opened a new window display of sweets in Clery's on O'Connell Street.

'I think it's because there's less work involved in them, less packaging. There's a slightly higher margin, if you can sell them.'

One story in particular provides a sign of how the new and the old have come to an accommodation.

'Our Aungier Street shop front is listed, and we try to keep with the old values but you have to try to survive. The crossing between the old time and the modern time came with a regular called Paddy who would have probably known my grandfather. He would come in and buy Condor tobacco. On this particular day, we had a Chinese girl called Grace working in the shop. I was working in the wee office at the back and one of the Polish guys came running in saying: "Eddie, Eddie, Eddie! Paddy is complaining." So I came running out and Paddy was there with his walking stick and a whole lot of customers listening to him. I said, "What's wrong, Paddy?" And he said he'd asked Grace for a packet of Condor and she'd given him a packet of condoms.

'I said: "I'm very sorry, Paddy."

He replied: "There's no need to apologise. I'm just happy she still thinks I'm sexually active."'

The world has changed beyond recognition, but, happily, the sweets remain the same.